Communicate!

Talking and Staying Close
with Youth in Today's Culture

Dr. John A. Gross

PRESS

Dedication

To my lovely wife Susan, my partner in ministry and life, so sharing and giving over these past fifty years (who always has a cheery smile and words of encouragement), my children, Tommy (and his wife Lynette), Debbie (and her husband Bill), and our four grandchildren, Tiffany, Parker, Heather, and Casie, And four great grandchildren, Ryan, Joshua, Noah, Joseph...
all who willingly gave time and loving encouragement for this project to Become a dream come true, I love you all very much.
Also, thank you to Cristy Merrel and Jan Kelley for sharing in gathering and working on much of the material presented.

Endorsements

John Gross has spent decades communicating biblical truth to a changing culture. He has never tried to change the message to match the culture. Rather he seeks to transform the culture through timeless truths rooted in God Himself. But how do we reach a millennial youth culture where the very existence of spiritual and moral truth is under question? Dr. Gross uses various surveys to give us a candid picture of desperate children in a climate of moral chaos. But he doesn't stop there. He goes on to show us how to fulfill the mandate of Deuteronomy 6:6-9 to instill biblical truth to our children in our homes, our churches, and our schools. Each chapter ends with practical questions and applications that challenge us to action. *Communicate!* is a very relevant book for anyone who is concerned about saving our children from a growing cesspool of violence, drugs, sexual perversion, and the destruction of the family unit.

Dr. Dave Anderson
Graduate Rice University, Ph.D. Dallas Seminary, President and Professor of Biblical Languages and Systematic Theology at Grace School of Theology.

I don't believe all the statistics that say 75% of millennia's are leaving the church. I think the problem is bad, but not what the secular press is telling us. John Gross has written this book to help Christians communicate with young people in their families and churches. He not only examines the problem, but offers many practical solutions. This book will help you to focus your ministry on reaching young people within your church and our culture.

Elmer L. Towns
Co Founder and Vice President, Liberty University
Liberty University | Training Champions for Christ since 1971

A barrier exists between today's youth who are crying out for help and adults who are available and equipped and who can provide the guidance needed to help them navigate the treacherous waters of teen life. In most cases parents and youth leaders are already on the scene to assist, but their youth cannot hear them—leaving both utterly frustrated

Dr. John Gross has successfully worked with youth, parents, pastors and youth leaders for several decades. His tenure as the President of Singing Hills Youth Camp near Albuquerque, New Mexico has placed him in direct contact with thousands of youth needing guidance who are now living productive lives. His book, "Communicate," is a comprehensive guide for parents and youth leaders who are committed to changing the lives of young men and women in their sphere of influence. He presents case studies, information, technique and exercises that are not only proven but simple to implement. I highly recommend this work as a must read for parents, teachers and youth workers in our era.

Dan Greer
MDiv, Pastor - Community Baptist Church,
The Woodlands, Texas

CONTENTS

Preface

There are several objectives involved when addressing the issue of communicating with today's youth and retaining them for tomorrow's church. The frustrations that confront today's ministries are varied, but most are found in the areas of communication and retention.

How do we communicate with today's youth? Why are we losing so many of our young people to the world if we are communicating the principles of God's Word? We are *not* communicating the message that produces values and principles. Many parents and youth leaders just do not have the skills needed to communicate these principles.

We not only need to know how to communicate, but we need to know the principles to communicate which will empower youth to gain character, stability, and consistency for their future years. Many of our youth are not developing their ability to maintain a Christian stance.

Retention is a matter of developing foundational values and principles that will automatically come into action when a decision is called for in time of challenge. Values need to be developed early in Christian life for proper character to be exercised as one matures and develops into early adulthood.

Throughout this project issues are developed which address these questions.

Methods and techniques are discussed which can be used by youth leaders to help better deal with the principal concern in:

(1) Communicating

(2) Retaining today's youth for tomorrow's church

Information presented will show where we have failed to communicate values and biblical principles and how we have failed to give our youth techniques to deal with their decision process. We will develop some "How to" methods of communication as well as some "How not to" methods of communication.

The purpose of this book is to provide our youth values and principles that will give them the ability to remain faithful to the cause of Christ, the church, and others.

We are facing the issue of destroyed foundations. We must realize that King David's words are as correct today as they were when he first asked, "If the foundations be destroyed, what can the righteous do?" (Psalm 11:3). **The biblical issue is the fact that the Word of God is absolute truth.** The values of truth, marriage, purity, honesty, love, peace, and happiness are values that must be built on the scriptural foundation of absolute truth. Accepting the biblical message of truth is the beginning point for teaching our youth the principles of life that will bring them fulfillment and happiness. If the Bible is not accepted as the authority by which lives and futures are built, it is difficult to bring about effective results in the aforementioned areas.

These subjects will be approached assuming the Word of God *is* accepted as the authority by which we draw our conclusions:

"Hear, O Israel: The LORD our God, the LORD *is* one!
You shall love the LORD your God with all your heart,
with all your soul, and with all your strength.
"And these words which I command you today shall be in your heart.
You shall
Teach them diligently to your children...."
(Deuteronomy 6:4-7a NKJV)

I started my research on communicating with youth over a decade ago, and it formed the basis of my dissertation. My life experience in ministry has validated the principles I knew then only as academic findings. My gut-level response was that they were practical and useful truths and principles of communication with ongoing application for the church. In revisiting my material, I have kept the meat and taken out the bones, so to speak. I am sharing contemporary statistics and findings that further expose the needs and cries for understanding and help from youth. It is my prayer that these findings and practical applications will strengthen, deepen, and make more effective your communication with youth in the family and church.

-Dr. John Gross
Houston, 2015

Introduction

The Importance of Communicating with Youth

This book is based on my observations as a pastor for over forty years as well as President of Singing Hills Youth Camp for over twenty years. Additional experience includes the direction of other programs relating to young people. I have held many one-on-one discussions as well as group meetings on this subject.

There exists a need for information that will help us more effectively communicate a message of victory and hope for the future lives of youth in the present age. The frustration comes from all directions. Many church youth leaders and senior pastors are concerned that so many young people do not attend church, nor are they involved from the time of their youth until they enter young adult and young married years.

I have expended much energy over the years to gather material from various sources of youth-minded ministries and individuals who have dedicated their entire lives to reach the youth of their generation.

Not until lately have there been effective surveys that acquired the facts concerning churched youth as well as unchurched youth. When one takes a hard look at the present surveys and facts now being produced, it becomes very evident that we have a problem in our retention and development programs that were designed to produce results. I am indebted to Luther Seminary for providing one of the most comprehensive lists of resources about youth that I have discovered. Appendix B provides this listing for you, the reader, so that you can find information about the issues most affecting the adults and youth that you are seeking to minister to and more effectively reach with communication.

One of the major problems in developing and producing the desired results in the lives of our youth is the lack of time spent teaching and training them godly character and morals.

This debate has gone on for several decades. The family is losing its influence to schools, government, and media. Young people are quick to tell you that it is no longer their parents who have the greatest impact or influence in their lives. It is interesting to find out who *is* having the most influence on youth and on their decisions for the future. Surprising as it may sound, the largest influence is other youth they are with every day. Mass media, schools, coaches, and peers are also having considerable influence on them. Why is the family losing ground while other forces are gaining greater control?

In his book, *The Future of the American Family,* George Barna helps us understand the dilemma families are facing.

How do you raise youth these days? The extended family generally is not available to lend a helping hand. In most households, both parents work. And who has the time to read Dr. Benjamin Spock's classic 800-page manual on child rearing?

While the public debate rages over who has the greatest influence on the development of our children, parents themselves offer some useful insights. For starters, we learned that three-quarters of all adults assert that "these days, most youth are influenced more by the schools, government, media, and other sources than they are by their parents." This is a sentiment echoed by many young people themselves.

Of course, most adults say that parents should have the most influence on their children. What may be most surprising, though, is whom parents identify as the single biggest influence on their youth: other youth. Other significant influences are parents and the mass media. Schools rate fourth. Churches and the government are rarely mentioned as having much influence.

Statistics like this certainly raise a long list of questions. Why aren't churches playing a bigger role in the process? What can be done to enhance the impact of parental influence? How can the influence of the media be moderated? What kind of values are being taught by those groups outside of the family? Although these complex questions are difficult to answer accurately, we must address them, for the implications are profound.

Those who warn that parents don't spend enough time inculcating values and sharing time with their families are often written off as ignorant fundamentalists, out-of-touch conservatives, or pontificating moralists. But their perspective, alarming and uncomfortable as it may be for some, cannot be easily dismissed, given the weight of the evidence that confirms their contention. For instance, a number of scholarly studies have noted youth draw most of their information from the television, spending an average of more than 10,000 hours watching it by the time they reach age eighteen. (That, by the way, represents more than one entire year—twenty-four-hour days, seven days a week—absorbing the messages broadcast by television producers.) The typical child in preschool through sixth-grade age group watches in excess of thirty hours of television programming per week.

Many adults seem baffled and even frustrated when trying to weigh the benefits and drawbacks of child care.

Further diminishing the input of parents is the extended time youth spend in school. The typical child in 1880 attended school 80 days per year;

today, most states have a school year that lasts about 180 days. Preschool experience used to be uncommon; today, six out of ten children attend preschool classes prior to enrolling in kindergarten.[1]

Building family relationships is one of our most urgent assignments, and it becomes one of the greatest challenges before us as we examine the matrix of problems facing our youth. Test scores show that our teens desire deeper relationships and more meaningful communication with their parents. So the challenge is how to develop deeper and more meaningful relationships?

Progression through this book will reveal the importance of learning communication skills and using them to impart acceptance, love, and respect to our youth.

The church has a tremendous challenge before it as it attempts to provide the programs that will address these questions and give answers to the problems that are plaguing our families and their teenagers.

> Ministries in the church that involve our youth have the responsibility to recognize the problem and to develop and give proper direction that could help solve the problems in today's society.

The challenge before the church is almost immeasurable. For example, Ron Hutchcraft states in an article in *Ministry Advantage:*

Statistics show that almost half the youth within today's North American church have had pre-marital sex by the age of 18. If you were to ask them what they believe, they would tell you the biblically correct answer. The inability to connect beliefs with actions is the dilemma for young people in the 90s. Students may agree with everything the Bible says, yet may fail to grow beyond surface- level Christianity.

When young people are challenged they often rise to the occasion. Under challenged students become expert sermon evaluators instead of faithful doers.

As long as students are merely entertained, they will become increasingly bored. The goal of discipleship is not right answers; it is understanding and obeying. You need to bring students into your daily routine to be a practical example of how to combine Christian beliefs with action.

General Christianity is largely empty Christianity. **Specific faith** connects beliefs with behavior.

1. **Specific Dedication.** Youth will love the Lord more when they give him something each day instead of trying to give everything all at once.

2. **Specific Prayer.** Ask students for prayer for specific people and things, not broad concepts. Teach them about specific praying to allow them to experience real answers from God.

3. **Specific Witness.** Every youth must have the name of at least one person he or she wants to take to Heaven. Show your youth group how to individualize their immediate mission field.

4. **Specific Repenting.** Don't have them repent of their "many sins." Encourage them to confess and repent of something with a specific name. Teach young people to make Jesus the Lord over something that has a name every day.[2]

Through the course of this book, it will be established that there exists a breakdown in parent/child communication. This can be established by simply reading the facts about where we are in our relationship with youth. Along with the recognition of breakdown, we must ask:

"How can I develop relationships and improve communication?"

Asking ourselves questions about our communicating with youth is mandatory for every teacher, preacher, coach, or parent. Reviewing methods and techniques of communication in the following chapters will inspire all of us to try harder to understand today's youth.

These are questions that many will not want to face, simply because it may mean taking the initiative to change, and it will mean recognizing mistakes. But most of all, it will move us closer in confronting and addressing issues that could ultimately have total victory for the future of our youth. If these issues are ignored, they will surely bring ultimate defeat. We will endeavor to give solutions that can be realized with the utmost confidence and assurance. When a parent or leader undertakes the responsibility of developing a means of communication and wants to motivate students to become productive and successful, he quickly reaches the conclusion that there's also a message to communicate. What is it? Not only "How do I do it?" but also "What is it that I need to be communicating that is going to produce the desired results?"

There are many messages that need to be given out, but as we will see in this book, the bottom line is that we must develop two major themes in the heart and mind of our youth. One will be that life needs to be based on that which is absolute. Foundational principles of absolute truth are the bedrock on which all other decisions are based. Therefore, we will seek to answer the twin questions, "What is truth?" and "What are the absolutes that result in making responsible decisions in life?"

Another very important factor is that we must develop in the hearts and minds of our youth who Jesus is and what He means to their lives. The fact is that Jesus is "the truth" and He is "the life." Truth is a person and that person is Jesus Christ. That is the absolute on which all of life is based. This foundation must be built if we are to have *real* communication with our youth.

There are many individuals who have committed themselves and their lives to reaching young people. Our hearts go out to them for their love and commitment. We must pray that the Lord of the harvest will continue to send forth laborers into these hungry, needy fields. Those who have dedicated and given themselves to the ministry of reaching and developing our youth are very special people. For their labor, we thank them and pray for the Lord's special blessings in their ministries. It is my desire that this book will provide teachers, parents, coaches, and friends of teenagers a special challenge and helpful information that will produce healthy and successful lives for the future ministries and professions of our youth.

In light of that I have included a small group interactive section at the end of each chapter to help you and your church better equip youth leaders, parents, and peer counselors to communicate with today's youth. If possible, ask your group to each have a copy of this book and to read the first chapter of this book prior to your first gathering.

PART I

DO WE HAVE A CRISIS?

Chapter 1

Yes, We Do Indeed Face a Crisis

The following news articles relate to some degree the severity of the crisis that confronts those who desire to challenge and reach our youth of today. As you read these true stories, I want to challenge you to remember that this occurred in a local neighborhood on the west side of Houston, not far from my church in the early 1990s. Then I will tell you a similar story still in Houston being played out more than a decade later.

I would remind you that these are young people who are attending a regular high school, just like the one in your neighborhood. These are teenagers who attend our churches and go to the football pep rallies, just as thousands of other teenagers in our cities. I would encourage you to realize that the following illustrations are being repeated across our country in alarming numbers. The question is, "Do we have a crisis on our hands?" After reading these articles and taking a hard look at the facts, I think we must all admit that, yes, we do indeed face a crisis in the lives of our youth and their futures.

Bear Creek Park

A 17-year-old accused of attacking another teen with a hatchet and leaving him to die in a wooded area of Bear Creek Park will stand trial for murder in adult court. State District Court Judge Robert Baum ruled Wednesday that Stanley Kazuo Nicholas will be tried as an adult in the death of Robbie Bayley, 18. No trial date has been scheduled. Nicholas remains in custody without bond.

This mid-July 1993 slaying was especially disturbing because teens in his west Harris County neighborhood knew Bayley had been killed; but kept the secret to themselves. A sixteen-year-old who had been present when Bayley was killed later led tours of the scene to show off the decomposing corpse.

The adult certification hearing ended Wednesday. Testimony a day earlier indicated that Nicholas bragged to friends of killing Bayley.

After the killing, Bayley's body lay near Langham Creek until mid-August, when two boys found the skeleton in a wooded area. Bayley's father and stepmother, Calvin and Wanda Bayley, had heard about the skeleton being found, but did not suspect it was their son. The teen had his own apartment and lived on his own. But when Bayley didn't call home on Sept. 8—his 19th birthday—his relatives became worried. They called many of his friends before one girl casually told them Bayley was dead, according to testimony.

The Bayleys then called police and reported their son missing. One day soon after, they got an anonymous call advising them to match their son's dental records with the skeleton found in the woods. The next day, the Harris County medical examiner's office confirmed that the skeleton was Bayley's.

Bayley's girlfriend, Kathy Gowen, tearfully testified that she last saw him when he left with Nicholas and a sixteen-year-old friend.

Robert Singleton, eighteen, who knew both Nicholas and Bayley, testified that he heard rumors first that Bayley was dead and then visited the body twice, once led by the sixteen-year-old. Nicholas, according to testimony, told Singleton he had killed Bayley because the victim had gotten some of Nicholas' friends in some unspecified trouble.

According to testimony, Bayley was lured into the woods by the sixteen-year-old with Nicholas trailing behind. Nicholas allegedly beat Bayley in the head with the hatchet, then threw it into a nearby bayou.[1]

As you read that account, I'm sure you found it to be one of the most astonishing and frightening things you ever read. These youth knew of this young man's death and his body was hidden in the woods for several days with the neighborhood youth well aware of the circumstances. While the parents were frantically searching for their son, the young people were taking their dates and viewing the body. To prove that they were at the scene of the murder, they (the youth with their dates) would take portions of the body back to show their peers that they had made the tour. Later articles indicated that, as the youth were asked why they did such a thing, their answer was, "Well, everybody else was doing it... it just seemed to be the thing to do."

Now, let's jump forward two decades to 2013, and look at a more recent news story.

HOUSTON-AREA HIGH CANCELS CLASSES REST OF WEEK. POSSIBLE GANG RIVALRY INVESTIGATED.

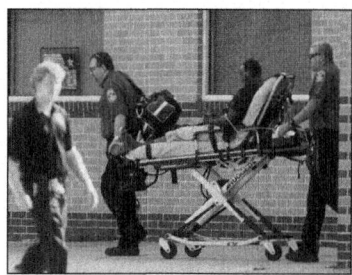

Emergency personnel remove a person from Spring High School in Spring, Texas, after at least one person was killed and others were injured during an altercation.(Photo: Mayra Beltran, AP)

A teen student was stabbed to death and three others were injured in a possible gang-related confrontation Wednesday at Spring High School in the Houston suburb of Spring, Texas, Harris County Sheriff Adrian Garcia said.

Three students described as "persons of interest" were taken into custody after the fight in a hallway leading to the school cafeteria, he said. At least two were taken away in handcuffs, KTRK-TV reports. The sheriff's office later said it was questioning a seventeen-year-old boy as the only suspect, the *Houston Chronicle* reported. Spring High School, which serves 3,000 students, was locked down, and classes were canceled the rest of the week.

Garcia said the stabbing occurred around 7:10 a.m. and "may have been gang-related." He said the incident started with a physical confrontation involving a "cutting instrument." Investigators have not found the weapons involved.

Authorities have not named the dead student, but several news reports identified him as Joshua Broussard, a seventeen-year-old sophomore.

KPRC-TV spoke with a man who said he was the father of the slain teen. "He was just trying to come to school today," he said of his son. The victim's aunt, who identified herself as Alisa Broussard, said the killing "was random."

The sheriff said two students were taken to the hospital with minor injuries and the third was undergoing surgery. KTRK-TV said one of the injured teens was stabbed in the abdomen and had been listed in critical condition at Memorial Hermann Hospital, but later his condition was upgraded to good. The TV station had previously quoted a family member as saying the boy was fighting for his life.

At midmorning, the school sent out an e-mail and recorded message to parents:

"This is an important message from Spring High School. Based on a preliminary report, a fight occurred this morning in the cafeteria. There has been one fatality and three students have been transported to hospitals with injuries. All other students are safe in their classrooms and will remain there while the investigation continues. Students will be released as soon as we have been given permission from the investigating authorities. We will call you again as soon as we have more details."

"When street violence pours into the schools, it compromises the well-being of all our students," said Ralph Draper, Spring ISD superintendent, at a news conference outside the school. "It is our aim to re-establish a safe and secure place for students on campus." He said police arrived on campus within 60 seconds of being summoned. Garcia said the campus has no metal detectors.

Pastor E.A. Deckard of Green House International Church told the *Houston Chronicle* that he was serving as spokesman for the family of one of the victims. Deckard said the incident was part of an ongoing battle involving young men of different races.

"We as a community need to come together to show kids the value of real life," Deckard said, adding that "this was not gang violence, but simply a misunderstanding between two people."

My City... Houston, Texas

It is hard to imagine that we are living in such cruel and unrelenting times. I grew up in a small West Texas town during the days of the "Oil Boom," when your name and your word were sealed with a handshake and "I'll pay you next week." This was a town where the shade trees overlapped the street, you never thought of locking your doors, the 5:00 p.m. whistle meant that Dad was coming home from work, Mother would have supper on the table in thirty minutes, and everybody had better be there (or you were in trouble).

Houston is a little different. I want you to read a 1994 article from the *Houston Chronicle*:

Harvesting Years of Neglect and Abuse

A boy named Juan munches on a hamburger by a busy street in Pasadena and says he doesn't remember a time when he wasn't fighting somebody. He is resigned to what he considers his destiny: to die on the streets or kill somebody there.

Jamie goes to work at a drugstore on the east side, his first legitimate job and one that pays a small fraction of what he made in the high-rolling days when he robbed and stole with abandon. He tries not to feel the tap of temptation on his shoulder.

Sweet-faced Bobby, experienced hijacker and himself long abused, stands smoking a cigarette outside his sister's Spring Branch apartment, the home they have made for themselves because their mother could not. The question lingers long after the smoke clears: Can you get the old neighborhood out of the boy as easily as the boy out of the neighborhood?

Eric, serious, seldom smiling, sits on a corner in decrepit Freedman's Town, smoking some weed with his homeboys and keeping an eye out for cops. He broods over his future. Will he have a life any better than that of the ex-slaves who laid these streets?

Four lines on a statistician's data entry. Four victims and four victimizers, each likable in one moment, threatening in the next. Four youth—angry, depressed, fearful, and wanting—the rechristened horsemen of the apocalypse.

One can try to understand the epidemic of violent juvenile crime through official pronouncements, screaming headlines, and talk-show hysteria. But to appreciate its full and frightening impact, one must come face-to-face with those responsible for the trend. Hearing their stories, listening to them talk, it becomes almost impossible to ignore what they are first and foremost: damaged children.

They have always been with us, but never have they reached such critical mass. Never have they been so mixed up with guns and drugs, so abused, so steeped in violence, so unprepared for a future. Never have they been so separated from mainstream culture that they did not believe in a future.

So, wide-eyed, we keep measuring their destructive capacity. The FBI, collector of nationwide statistics, reports a 47 percent increase in violent crime arrests of those under eighteen from 1988 to 1992. In Texas over the same time, the jump was 131 percent. In Harris County, juvenile probation officials stagger under the weight of a load they would not have imagined a decade ago. Referrals for serious felony offenses went from just under 3,000 in 1985 to more than 5,000 last year.

With the rise in young criminals came a rise in young victims. Nearly one in four violent crimes involved juvenile victims in 1992, up from one in five in 1987, according to a recently released Department of Justice report. The chances of being a victim of a violent crime was more than five times greater for those 12 to 17 than for people 35 or older. One of every 13 juveniles was a violent crime victim in 1992.

The explosion of youthful crime and violence has set off an avalanche of publicity, so much that a recent story about the murder of a Houston store manager by a teen who wanted a pair of athletic shoes was deemed routine and awarded all of five paragraphs. The bigger stories are set off by a higher—or is it lower?—level of inhumanity, though not by any more insight. Between the horrible deed and the staccato accounts of it, the perpetrator's identity is lost.

In the case of young people, our difficulty in separating the crime from the criminal leads us down a strange and some would say dangerous path. Because their acts are "worthy" of an adult, we strive to treat them as such.

We argue, through our legislators, that the age for being shunted into the adult criminal system be lowered to 14, 13, 12... Barring that, the best thing we can do is build more juvenile prisons, more detention centers, and more boot camps.

The upcoming governor's race threatens to become an exercise in tough rhetoric. Who can serve up the meanest sound bite? Who can swing the biggest paddle? George W. Bush already has accused Gov. Ann Richards of being soft on juvenile criminals. Conspicuously absent is discussion of how to influence children and families before their problems get severe.

"When youth walk off the cliff, our way of dealing with it is to build a prison at the bottom of the cliff, when we need to build a fence at the top," said Steve Robinson, executive director of the Texas Youth Commission, which handles the state's toughest young offenders. "Nobody seems to be in control of the front end of the system."

There is more than a whiff of machismo at work. It's easier to be angry than smart. Said state Rep. Allen Hightower, D-Huntsville, vice chairman of the Texas Commission on Children and Youth: "You're somehow less of a Texan if you're not for punishment, as opposed to fixing the behavior that led to the problem."

Ernest McMillan, founder of a prevention program in the Fifth Ward that tries to do exactly that, calls the repeated emphasis on enhancing punishment for juvenile offenders "a kind of insanity." Our desire for immediate gratification and for revenge is met, he said, but the underlying problems go unaddressed.

From the offices of the Harris County Juvenile Probation Department, where she works as staff psychiatrist, Ninfa Cavazos agrees completely.

"We can build more jails," she said, "until half of Houston is in jails and the rest of us are heavily taxed. We're propagating our own self-destruction."[2]

Again, let's jump ahead almost two decades and see if the story line has changed:

Houston Chronicle

TEEN CONVICTED OF
CAPITAL MURDER IN SATANIC KILLING

By Brian Rogers | December 11, 2014 | Updated

Teen on trial for 15-year-old girl's gruesome killing. Jose E. Reyes is one of the teens prosecutors accuse of kidnapping, sexually assaulting, and killing Corriann Cervantes, 15, because they wanted to sell their souls to the devil. A Harris County jury on Thursday convicted 18-year-old Jose E. Reyes of capital murder in a death tied to a satanic ritual, agreeing with prosecutors that another crime was committed when Corriann Cervantes was brutally killed.

Reyes was automatically sentenced to life in prison. Jurors took a little more than an hour to reach a decision, rejecting arguments from defense attorneys that if Reyes was guilty of a crime, it would be murder.

Moments after the verdict was announced in the courtroom, Cervantes' aunt, Michelle Abernathy, said she blamed Reyes and his parents for the death of her 15-year-old niece. Abernathy dressed down Reyes, saying he is "morally, spiritually dead."

Jurors agreed with prosecutors, who sought a conviction on a charge of capital murder. Earlier Thursday, prosecutors said in closing arguments that Reyes' own words prove he killed a girl because he wanted to sell his soul to the devil.

As you read through these stories, you had to ask yourself: "What can be done?" "What is the answer?" "Where have we gone wrong?" These are not easy questions nor are there easy answers. But the questions must be considered as we face the issues.

Communication and Retention Action Steps

If the foundation be destroyed, what can the righteous do? (Psalm 11:3)

One of the major problems in developing and producing the desired results in the lives of our youth is the lack of time spent teaching and training them godly character and morals.

We not only need to know how to communicate, but we need to know the principles to communicate which will empower youth to gain character, stability, and consistency for their future years.

These communication and retention action steps have been designed to help youth leaders, parents, and peers establish these missing foundations and give practical suggestions on how to bring about real change in our churches, communities, and cities.

Preparation:

Begin by asking yourself:

What is it that I need to be communicating to produce the desired results?

How am I going to build this firm foundation in my own life first?

How can I make my own life a better model for the young people in my life to emulate?

Read 2 Timothy 2:15-18.

What do you need to personally do to obey this scripture?

Pray and ask God to show you how to rightly handle His Word and His principles as you work with the leaders and parents of teens and young people.

Communication:

Ask your group to read the articles in this chapter:

What values and biblical principles were not communicated that would have helped these youth deal with their decision process?

Ask your group how they would explain "You shall not kill" is one of the Ten Commandments (Exodus 20:13).

Does God value everyone's life?

Ask them to explain their answer.

Read what Jesus said in Matthew 10:29-30.

Ask them to explain what they think this means.

Ask them how they would explain to teens how God feels about one person killing another person.

Read Leviticus 24:21b.

What does this tell us about what God thinks about one person murdering another?

Read 1 John 3:15.

> *Why is it important to understand this principle?*
> *What does hate breed in our hearts and minds?*
> *Discuss how we can help our young people deal with the hate*
> *they see in the world around them.*

Retention:

- *Have your youth leaders and parents to go through the newspaper or watch news reports and evaluate what they are reading about other young people in their area for the next week.*

- *Have them begin to keep a journal of what they read and what foundational godly truth they feel was not taught to the young person who committed the crime in the story.*

- *Ask them to bring their journals with them to your next meeting and be prepared to discuss their findings.*

- *Have them read the next chapter before your next meeting.*

Chapter 2

Statistics Confirm that Youth Are Crying Out for Help— Where Is the Church?

The material in the previous chapter has made it evident that we have a tremendous problem. Our youth are searching for meaning in life and at times may be out of control during those years. Our challenge is to impart a relevant faith to carry them into adulthood as leaders of tomorrow's church. What this book will be doing is overviewing the material that identifies the spiritual health of the Millennials with this primary question in mind: *What can we learn from Millennials (ages 18-29) that we can use to reach the current generation of teenagers (ages 12-18) in the church with the gospel, Good News of Great Joy, in relevant, practical and impactful ways?* Barna research has given us much insight on Millennials. I want to summarize it for you and define certain themes we need to follow throughout this book as we uncover effective ways to communicate and share the Gospel with Millennials.

The Spiritual Journeys of Millennials

One important item to recognize is the rise of the unaffiliated, faithless "Nones." The term "Nones" is being used to describe the number of Americans who claim to have no faith or say they are unaffiliated with any belief system.[1] Each survey used to identify the "Nones" conveys that a significant number of "Millennials" are identified with the "Nones." The first survey found that nearly one third of the Millennial Generation was identified with the "Nones."[2] Who are these faithless twenty-somethings? Where did they come from? Did they ever claim to have faith? What is it about religion that has left them cold?

These Millennial "Nones" may have come from your church or a church similar to yours. Many, about eight million, would have professed faith at one time. It is the third question that is difficult to answer. If the Church is to "make disciples" of our youth, the third question, "what is it about religion that has left them cold," must be answered. Once the answer is given, the Church must not file it away, but must respond. May the Lord use this book to help provide answers and responses to the third question!

As we continue, let us understand that each of us is on "a spiritual journey." None of us are where we started nor at the destination. We are in the midst of the journey. So too, each of the Millennials identified as a "None" is on a spiritual journey. According to David Kinnaman, president of the Barna Group, in his book *You Lost Me*, the once churched Millennial is on a spiritual journey typified by one of these three terms: "nomads," "prodigals" and

---

[1]   The term rose to prominence when a Pew Research poll found that the number of Americans who are religiously unaffiliated rose to almost 20%—a nearly 5% leap in just the last five years. In the subsequent months, a Gallup poll showed similar numbers, and most recently, in March 2013, a poll from UC-Berkeley and Duke University similarly found religious affiliation in the U.S. is at its lowest point since it began to be tracked.

[2]   The Pew Research Poll

"exiles." These terms define groups based upon common answers to a variety of questions about religious belief and attitudes toward Christianity, churches and faith. Their answers may provide an answer and a proper response to the third question "what is it about religion that has left them cold?"

Nomads

A nomad is a person who has no fixed home but wanders from place to place. For centuries there have been desert people groups who have travelled from water hole to water hole and sheep herders who have travelled from pasture to pasture. The wandering from place of sustenance to place of sustenance that characterizes nomads of the desert typifies a large segment of the "Millennial" generation. These spiritual "Nomads" have difficulty settling down and identifying with the "institutional" church or a "brand" of Christianity. You may identify them as "church hoppers."

These "nomads" consider themselves Christian. They see themselves as personally interested in God and religion. But they are not interested in a formal or institutionalized expression of that faith. This disinterest may arise from experiences with formal and / or institutionalized situations. These Nomads often believe that the church attendance and Christian friends are optional.

Christianity for these "Nomads" is intensely personal. The intensely personal nature of their Christianity usually focuses on their personal interest and relationship with God. They would probably claim to love Jesus and speak of their "personal relationship" with Him. From the church's perspective, they are wanderers, "Nomads," but they would never claim to have lost their faith.

Prodigals

Prodigals are people who have lost their faith. These Millennials, at one time, claimed to have a personal faith, but they no longer make that profession. Many not only have lost their faith, but also claim they will never return to faith. What are some of the factors that have driven them from faith?

- Christian doctrine does not make sense.
- Experience(s) with other professing Christians or in the church have been negative.
- Their personal spiritual needs cannot be met by Christianity.

The "Prodigals" are the people who are usually identified with the "Nones." A "Prodigal" may not be opposed to faith or spirituality. But either a negative experience or intellectual response presents an imposing stumbling block resulting in leaving the Christian faith.

The Barna Group shows that one fifth of Millennials have problems with the Christian "belief system," a negative experience, or Christianity fails to meet their needs.

Exiles

An Exile has a Christian background is interested in maintaining their Christian faith, but is having difficulty living their faith, as expressed in the church in their day to day activities. Some would even say that, even though they still attend church, it is easier to live their faith day to day than in the church. An Exile wants to follow Jesus on a day to day basis, connecting their faith to the world around them. In their view, the church is "out of touch" with the World. In support of this, many Exiles observe that God is more active outside the church than inside the church. Those who make this observation want to be a part of what God is doing.

Hope Provides Opportunity

The "Nomads," "Prodigals," and "Exiles" are in conflict with churches and Christianity. That they are in conflict is hopeful. They are concerned about faith, connection, and want to be involved. Being involved with the church provides many Millennials with a sense of excitement. A sizable portion (better than 2 in 5) express concern that their generation is leaving the church. The same portion claim they want a "traditional" faith and not a "hip" faith. Yet, as the previous graphs show, we need to recognize the sobering reality that many Millennials, having grown up in the church, are going or have gone through a period of rejecting the church and the faith they were taught. They may be holding on to the faith while rejecting the church. They may have rejected the church and the faith. Or they may be wrestling with connecting faith and culture. How can the church respond? What are the reasons the Millennial Generation has conflicts with the church and faith?

"Walking in the Shoes" of the Millennials

Mark Twain wrote *The Prince and the Pauper*. It is said that the Iroquois said that before you can judge another you have to walk a mile in his moccasins. Both Twain and the Iroquois understood that understanding another involved learning to see things from another's perspective. The church needs to apply that principle and listen to the Millennial Generation. What are the Millennials communicating? What do we think we understand that is not true? The Barna Group spent sixteen months touring the nation listening to Millennials. The national tour, *You Lost Me, Live,* provided opportunities for leaders, pastors, and parents to listen. A host of Millennials told of their spiritual journeys and views.

Those who listened heard that the Millennial Generation is a homeless generation. They are wanderers. This characteristic is a result of the Millennials putting off marriage, children, and other "adult" responsibilities. They want to explore, take risks, be participants, and be free to be spontaneous. In their wandering, they desire to be loyal to their "fellow travellers," the other members of their generation.

The characteristics of exploration, risk taking, spontaneity, participation, and membership in the "Millennial Tribe" have produced a spiritual "homelessness" resulting in the "Nomad," "Prodigal," and "Exile." Consequently, they see the "normal" church experience as sedate, non-spontaneous, insular, and featureless. These wanderers want roots, but not roots for the sake of preserving what does not belong to them.

The church needs to listen to and communicate with the Millennial Generation, to "speak their language." In doing so, the Millennial Generation

> The wise church leadership will draw the Millennial into the process of "doing church."

needs to be challenged to become part of the church community by becoming valued members of the community that they help create. They must be invited by the church community to help shape a spiritual home.

How can your church include the Millennial? If the Millennial Generation is to be invited to help shape the spiritual community, what do we need to know so that we can communicate? How can the invitation be presented so that it is genuine and perceived to be genuine? The Barna group conducted a five year study that resulted in David Kinnaman's book *You Lost Me: Why Young Christians are Leaving Church and Rethinking*

Church. This book identifies six reasons the Millennial Generation wanders from the church and becomes spiritually homeless.

1. **The Church is a Cocoon.** The world of today is a world of information. The Millennial Generation has never known a world without the internet. Communication with others throughout the world can be instantaneous. Communication is also often cryptic and "coded" as in LOL means "laugh out loud" and not "little old lady" or "lots of love." The Millennials want to connect their faith in Christ to this world. They perceive that the church ignores the world's problems, focuses on what is "wrong" with the world, and generally condemns everything outside the church. Therefore the Millennial Generation sees the church as opposed to risk, fearful, and stifling. This view of the church is contrary to the Millennial desire to be adventuresome, spontaneous, and exploratory.

2. **The Church is a "baby pool."** The Millennial Generation wants to swim. There are lakes, rivers, and even oceans that beckon, but the church is a backyard pool for babies. The World beckons, entices, and excites. The church is "boring." From week to week, the church goes through predictable motions and from year to year presents traditional programs. The Millennial finds career and interests more interesting and exciting than church. Actually, for many, the church is irrelevant. As a generation, the Millennial Generation is one of the most educated generations. They are accustomed to learning: new tasks, new hobbies, new exercises, new recipes, etc. But the church, in their view, fails to teach the Bible clearly or sufficiently. Sadly, in the baby pool of the church, God seems to be missing. It is in the lakes, rivers, and oceans of the World that many of the Millennials "experience" and / or need God.

3. **The Church is not a Laboratory.** The Millennial generation is familiar with the "scientific method." Chemistry, physics, biology, and other fields of study have exposed them to "proofs," experimentation, and the concept that man, through research, is able to address and eventually solve his problems. The church is perceived as opposed to science and made up of people who "have all the answers." The world is driven to technologic heights through science and the church is "out of step." Consequently, the "evolution – creation" debate is tiresome and irrelevant. The "oil and water" relationship between the church and science places many young science-minded Millennials on the horns of a dilemma. How can a person maintain their faith and maintain their integrity as a professional in science related industries?

4. **The Church is "Puritanical" and "Victorian."** The Millennial Generation lives in a world of sexual enticement, overload, and availability. Many professing to be Christians are as involved in sexual activity as those who do not make the same profession. The ubiquitous sexual enticements and the church's expectation of sexual purity and chastity produce high levels of tension for those who put off marriage until the late twenties. The problem is made worse when the sexual activity of the unmarried is "discovered" by the church and the church "judges" and "condemns." The issue of sexual involvement is particularly salient when sexual activity and birth control are condemned "out of hand." This type of condemnation is seen as being out of date, and irrelevant to the "real world."

5. **The Church is a "Private Club."** The Millennial Generation has been shaped by a culture that values tolerance, acceptance, and open minds. It is the most eclectic generation in American history in terms of race, ethnicity, sexuality, religion, technological tools,

and sources of authority. Consequently many Millennials look for common ground with others often at the expense of ignoring significant differences. Often this means that a young person feels that a choice must be made between "faith and friends." The Millennials, who enjoy exploring and taking risks, sense that the church is fearful of other faith systems. The desire to find common ground and integrating faith with friends gives the Millennial the impression that the church is a private club to which he / she does not wish to belong.

6. **The Church forbids Questions.** The Millennial has many questions not knowing how faith and culture fit together, nor how to be an explorer or risk taker within the church. In the experience of many, the church is not a safe place to ask questions. If the church listens to the question, the church's answer often communicates that the question was not taken seriously or becomes an avenue of judgment. Sadly, too many Millennials from a church background say that their faith does not address their depression or other emotional problems. If the Church does not answer their questions, to whom should they go?

The Need for Providing a Home, a Safe Place

The "Nomads," "Prodigals," and "Exiles" need a home, a safe place to be spontaneous, exploratory, and risk taking. They need a place that lets questions "hang in the air," that helps them negotiate the bumps, twists, turns, and detours in their life journey. The "traditional" Millennial, not in the majority, is generally content with the "traditional" church. But those who do not get married, find a career path, leave home, and enter into the expected "norms" of adult life by age thirty need to sense that the Church is able to provide them with roots, safety, and community. How can the Church provide the necessary community in the World of the Millennial that is ever changing, high tech, with many voices of authority?

The Church must avoid two responses. The first response is not to take the concerns of the Millennial Generation seriously, thinking that the expressed concerns are but a "phase." The second response is to focus on the millennial Generation and build the Church around their concerns. The first erroneous response ignores the great changes in our culture that impinge upon a Millennial's worldview. The church must seek to see things as the Millennial sees them. The second response ignores all those in the church who are not Millennials. This response ignores the biblical model of the Church as a body. The Millennials may be the legs or feet, but they are not the whole. The pursuit of the Church is to do the will of the "head," that is Christ. His will is that the whole of the body be involved and working together.

The biblical model of a body provides us with a picture that ought to help the Church provide roots, a safe haven, and community to the "Nomads," Prodigals," and "Exiles."

If your physical body has an itch, or infection, you scratch or apply medicine as necessary. You do not ignore the itch or infection nor do you ignore the needs of the rest of the body as you scratch or apply the necessary medicine. Many Church communities approach the questions and issues raised by the Millennial Generation in a "top down" manner. This manner is more in tune with the corporate world than with the body as described in the New Testament. The image of the body, as it pertains to the Church, suggests that addressing the issues of the Millennial Generation needs to be intergenerational. The Church is to function as a whole. If one portion of the Church itches or is infected, the whole of the Church is affected and should respond. The rest of this book will provide information describing the depth of the problem and give counsel regarding a biblical response to the problem.

Violence: The most visible and devastating symptom of the Communication Problem

The most current research completed on youth violence in the United States is staggering:

1. Youth in the U.S. are being killed in record numbers. Teenage boys in all racial and ethnic groups are more likely to die from gunshot wounds than from all natural deaths combined.
2. In 2006, among students ages 12-18, there were about 1.7 million victims of nonfatal crimes at school, including 909,500 thefts and 767,000 violent crimes.
3. In 2007, 36 percent of students in grades 9-12 reported they had been in a fight.
4. Persons under the age of 25 accounted for nearly 50 percent of those arrested for murder and 62 percent of those arrested for robbery in 2005.
5. Teen violence costs the United States approximately $158 billion each year in indirect and direct costs.

The evidence on teen violence is shocking. To reduce the financial strain and negative effects of teen violence, it is imperative to start now to break the cycle with young populations. Work towards reducing teen violence can be accomplished by delivering programs that create positive youth development.

What's Being Done

Youth violence prevention programs today seek to identify "risk" factors that increase risk for violence and "protective" factors that moderate that risk. Many programs are specifically developed to talk directly about youth violence and the do's and do not's rather than taking a broader approach and teaching lessons such as core competencies of social skills, asset-building, confidence, and decision-making.

The lack of social skills programming is important as it relates to brain functioning. Brain research has shown that different stages of the life cycle are sensitive periods for non-cognitive skills. Those sensitive periods to learn social skills and core competencies of self-regulation, values, communication skills, and positive identity come early in childhood and then again into adolescence.

Although many early childhood initiatives are available to develop non-cognitive skills, there is a gap between early childhood and the teenage years in the type of non-cognitive programming that is offered. The early childhood programs focus on cultivating necessary skills to make good choices and decisions, develop positive social skills, and nurture development. These programs with young children have been proven to reduce problem behaviors with those at risk. For youth, however, more emphasis is placed upon academics and grades.

Currently, public policy in the U.S. focuses on promoting and measuring cognitive ability through IQ and achievement tests. The accountability standards in the No Child Left Behind Act concentrate attention on achievement test scores and do not evaluate important non-cognitive factors that promote success in school and life. Though academics and achievement are important factors in child and youth development, research is showing that more than grades and academic knowledge, social skills, positive values and motivation are vital in preventing problem behavior and delinquency with individuals.[3]

Our young people need a balance of knowledge,
understanding, and wisdom.

Knowledge is information, understanding is how to apply this informa-tion, and wisdom tells them when and where to apply it.

Communication and Retention Action Steps

Preparation:

Begin by asking yourself:

What can I learn from Millennials (ages 18-29) *that I can use to reach the current generation of teenagers* (ages 12-18) *in the church with the gospel in relevant, practical, and impactful ways?*

Am I listening to and learning to speak their language?

How can help my church include the Millennial?

How can the invitation be presented so that it is genuine and perceived to be genuine?

Do I allow them to ask me questions or am I threatened when they do?

Read Hebrews 5:12-13.

---

[3] (http://wymancenter.org/wordpress/wp-content/uploads/2011/08/TOP-Teen-Violence.pdf)

> *What can I personally do to make this principle relevant to*
> *the Millennial?*

Read James 1:5-8.

Pray and ask God to give you the wisdom you need to impart His plan and purpose to each leader and parent who has a Millennial to reach.

Communication:

Nomads, prodigals, and exiles are terms used to define groups based upon common answers to a variety of questions about religious belief and attitudes toward Christianity, churches, and faith.

Use these phrases to begin a discussion on the groups discussed in this chapter.

Nomads might also be called _____.

Prodigals have problems with the Christian _____ _____, a _____ experience, or Christianity fails to _____ _____ _____.

Ask them if Millennials they know that do not attend church feel the church is "out of touch" with the World.

Do they feel God seems to be more active outside the church than inside the church?

Ask them how the church can change this perception?

Review the six reasons the Millennial Generation wanders from the church and becomes spiritually homeless. Ask them which ones they have heard expressed among their youth.

Then discuss how to openly answer each of these concerns.

1. **The Church is a Cocoon.** They perceive that the church ignores the world's problems, focuses on what is "wrong" with the world, and generally condemns everything outside the church.

2. **The Church is a "baby pool."** The church is boring and irrelevant. They are accustomed to learning new tasks, new hobbies, new exercises, new recipes, etc. but in their view the church fails to teach the Bible clearly or sufficiently.

3. **The Church is not a Laboratory.** The church is perceived as opposed to science and made up of people who "have all the answers." The world is driven to technologic heights through science and the church is "out of step." Consequently, the "evolution – creation" debate is tiresome and irrelevant.

4. **The Church is "Puritanical" and "Victorian."** The Millennial Generation lives in a world of sexual enticement, overload, and availability. The problem is made worse when the sexual activity of the unmarried is "discovered" by the church and the church "judges" and "condemns" which is seen as being out of date, and irrelevant to the "real world."

5. **The Church is a "Private Club."** The Millennial Generation has been shaped by a culture that values tolerance, acceptance, and open minds. Millennials look for common ground with others often at the expense of ignoring significant differences. Often this means that a young person feels that a choice must be made between "faith and friends" which gives the Millennial the impression that the church is a private club to which he / she does not wish to belong.

6. **The Church forbids Questions.** The Millennial has many questions not knowing how faith and culture fit together, nor how to be an explorer or risk taker within the church. In the

experience of many, the church is not a safe place to ask questions. Sadly, too many Millennials from a church background say that their faith does not address their depression or other emotional problems.

Retention:

Suggest your group conduct their own survey among their youth. Have them compile their own study using the nomad, prodigal, and exile categories presented in this chapter.

Have them ask their youth how they feel about the six reasons Millennials find church irrelevant.

Have them ask for suggestions as to how the church could respond

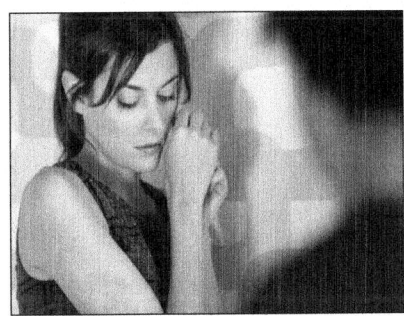

to bring relevance back into their local church.

Ask them to bring their survey results back to the next meeting.

Have them read the next chapter before your next meeting.

Chapter 3

Results of Failed Communication

𝒥 have selected for you a sampling of the results of poor communication with youth in our culture. First, read for yourself some of this tragic material and then I will disclose what I believe it tells us regarding communication challenges we have with our youth in the church.

Violence Didn't Drop Out of the Sky at Age Fifteen

"The latest research has found worryingly high levels of violence in young people's relationships," writes Christine Barter, NSPCC Senior Researcher at the University of Bristol (January 25, 2013 in Community Care).

Image credit: Garo/Phanie/Rex Features

Domestic violence is now recognized as constituting a major risk to the welfare of adult women and their children. However, violence in teenage relationships has failed, until recently, to receive the same level of attention.

The Latest Research Findings

Two recent research studies, undertaken by my colleagues and me, provide unequivocal evidence about the significance of this issue for the welfare of young people, and the wellbeing of girls and young women in particular. The initial study (Barter et al, 2009) surveyed more than 1,300 pupils aged 13 to 17 years and interviewed 90 young people. The research found worryingly high levels of violence in young people's relationships. A quarter of girls reported physical violence from a partner and a third had been pressured or forced into unwanted sexual acts. In comparison, 18 percent of boys reported some form of physical violence and 16 percent stated they had experienced sexual violence.

Many of the young women reported very high levels of control and surveillance from their partners, and once impact is also included, the gendered nature of this form of intimate violence becomes apparent. The majority of girls who experienced violence or control reported a negative impact on their welfare, including being scared, upset and humiliated. In comparison, boys reported being annoyed or no impact. Young people with a same-sex partner were also shown to be at risk of intimate violence.

A follow-up qualitative study (Wood et al, 2010) explored the issue with more disadvantaged groups, including young people in foster care and young mothers. Young women in this research reported substantially higher levels of partner violence compared to the first study, with the violence being more severe and frequent. Young mothers reported especially high levels of violence from their male partners, increasing during pregnancy and after the baby was born.

Many disadvantaged young people felt that violence was a normal, although unwelcome, aspect of being in a relationship. Worryingly, the vast majority of young people in both studies did not divulge their experiences to adults, including professionals. A range of associated risk factors were identified including: having experienced domestic violence or child abuse; associating with peers who use intimidation; and having a much older partner (at least two years older).

The impact of the research findings on social work practice

- There is a need to include an exploration of this form of violence as a routine aspect of all work with young people, even if it is not overtly apparent.
- Social workers should be aware that disadvantaged young people may have multiple risk factors in their lives which require addressing.
- Work with young women needs to include building self-esteem away from relationships.

Key issues for practitioners

- To ensure that violence in young people's relationships is viewed as being as serious as adult domestic violence.
- To develop expertise in working with young people in this sensitive area, including an awareness of possible risk factors.

- The need to counteract the negative view of professional support some young people hold – especially from young mothers.

Further Reading

Barter, C. (2009), In the Name of Love; Exploitation and violence in teenage dating relationships', *British Journal of Social Work, 39(2), p211-232*

Wood, M., Barter, C., and Berridge, D. (2010), Disadvantaged young people and partner violence, London, NSPCC

Community Care Inform guides to, and research related to, domestic violence

http://www.communitycare.co.uk/2013/01/25/how-the-latest-re-search-on-violence-in-teenage-relationships-should-inform-social-work-practice/

Understanding Youth Violence

Fact Sheet 2012

Youth violence refers to harmful behaviors that can start early and continue into young adulthood. The young person can be a victim, an offender, or a witness to the violence.

Youth violence includes various behaviors. Some violent acts—such as bullying, slapping, or hitting—can cause more emotional harm than physical harm. Others, such as robbery and assault (with or without weapons), can lead to serious injury or even death.

Why is youth violence a public health problem?

Youth violence is widespread in the United States (U.S.). It is the second leading cause of death for young people between the ages of 15 and 24.[1]

- 4,828 young people aged 10 to 24 were victims of homicide—an average of 13 each day—in 2010.[1]

- Over 707,000 young people aged 10 to 24 years had physical assault injuries treated in U.S. emergency departments in 2011—an average of 1,938 each day.[1]

- In a 2011 nationwide survey, about 33% of high school students reported being in a physical fight in the 12 months before the survey.[2]

- About 5% of high school students in 2011 reported taking a weapon to school in the 30 days before the survey.[2]

- In 2011, 20% of high school students reported being bullied on school property and 16% reported being bullied electronically.[2]

- Each year, youth homicides and assault-related injuries result in an estimated $16 billion in combined medical and work loss costs.[1]

How does youth violence affect health?

Deaths resulting from youth violence are only part of the problem. Many young people need medical care for violence-related injuries. These injuries can include cuts, bruises, broken bones, and gunshot wounds. Some injuries, like gunshot wounds, can lead to lasting disabilities.

Violence can also affect the health of communities. It can increase health care costs, decrease property values, and disrupt social services.[3]

Who is at risk for youth violence?

A number of factors can increase the risk of a youth engaging in violence. However, the presence of these factors does not always mean that a young person will become an offender.

Risk factors for youth violence include:

- *Prior history of violence*
- *Drug, alcohol, or tobacco use*
- *Association with delinquent peers*
- *Poor family functioning*
- *Poor grades in school*
- *Poverty in the community*

Note: This is a partial list of risk factors. For more information see Injury Prevention and Control Division of Violence Prevention.

Understanding Youth Violence

How can we prevent youth violence?

The ultimate goal is to stop youth violence before it starts. Several prevention strategies have been identified.

- Parent-based programs improve family relations. Parents receive training on child development. They also learn skills for talking with their kids and solving problems in nonviolent ways. In other words, communication is at the top of the prevention list.

- Social-development strategies teach children how to handle tough social situations. They learn how to resolve problems without using violence.

- Mentoring programs pair an adult with a young person. The adult serves as a positive role model and helps guide the young person's behavior.

- Changes can be made to the physical and social environment. These changes address the social and economic causes of violence.

How does CDC approach prevention?

The Center for Disease Control uses a four-step approach to address public health problems like youth violence.

Step 1: Define the problem

Before we can prevent youth violence, we need to know how big the problem is, where it is, and who it affects. CDC learns about a problem by gathering and studying data. These data are critical because they help us know where prevention is most needed.

Step 2: Identify risk and protective factors

It is not enough to know that youth violence is affecting a certain group of children in a certain area. We also need to know why. CDC conducts and supports research to answer this question. We can then develop programs to reduce or get rid of risk factors and increase protective factors.

Step 3: Develop and test prevention strategies

Using information gathered in research, CDC develops and evaluates strategies to prevent youth violence.

Step 4: Ensure widespread adoption

In this final step, CDC shares the best prevention strategies. CDC may also provide funding or technical help so communities can adopt these strategies.

For a list of CDC activities, see *Preventing Youth Violence: Program Activities Guide* (www.cdc.gov/violenceprevention/pub/preventingyv.html).

Where can I learn more?

Centers for Disease Control and Prevention

www.cdc.gov/violenceprevention

CDC Facebook Page on Violence Prevention

www.facebook.com/vetoviolence

STRYVE

www.vetoviolence.org/stryve/home.html

Stop Bullying

www.stopbullying.gov

Surgeon General's Report on Youth Violence

www.surgeongeneral.gov/library/youthviolence

References

1. Centers for Disease Control and Prevention, National Center for Injury Prevention and Control. Web-based Injury Statistics Query and Reporting System (WISQARS) [online]. (2010) [cited 2012 Oct 19]. Available from www.cdc.gov/ injury/wisqars.

2. Centers for Disease Control and Prevention. Youth risk behavior surveillance—United States, 2011. MMWR, Surveillance Summaries 2012; 61(no. SS-4).

3. Mercy J, Butchart A, Farrington D, Cerdá M. Youth violence. In: Krug E, Dahlberg LL, Mercy JA, Zwi AB, Lozano R, editors. The World Report on Violence and Health. Geneva, Switzerland: World Health Organization; 2002. p. 25–56.
   1-800-CDC-INFO (232-4636) • cdcinfo@cdc.gov • www.cdc.gov/ violenceprevention

Based on the Research and Statistics, Here's What We Have Learned About the Issues We Have Communicating with Youth.

I know you have seen the headlines and heard commentators and leaders from religious, political, law enforcement, community agencies, and various other backgrounds talk about the problem. I have given you these selected statistics just to refresh your memory of how broad and deep the challenges are in working with youth. As I read these alarming stories and stats, here is what I want you to know about the communication problems we have in our churches and culture as revealed by these facts:

1. Our youth do not value themselves nor do they believe others value them.

2. "More is Caught than Taught." Young people can spot a phony a "mile away." If you are going to communicate anything of God's grace, you must be gracious.

3. Our youth must learn that, in a world of change and upheaval, there is certainty and changelessness.

4. The Church must learn the language of the Youth if what is being said is to be understood.

5. The Church must not be content with addressing symptoms but must address the "root."

Communication and Retention Action Steps

Preparation:

Begin by asking yourself:

How did I feel when I read these statistics?

What did I learn about teen violence?

Am I willing to research this problem and find out what I can do to help change these alarming numbers?

How can I show these young people that I am not a fake and that I truly value them?

Read Psalm 119:1-11.

What important principles do I need to impart to the youth within my sphere of influence to help them not become a statistic in teen violence?

How can I help other leaders reach our youth and prevent teen violence in our area?

Pray using Psalm 119:33-37.

Communication:

Discuss implementing some of the CDC activities available at *Preventing Youth Violence: Program Activities Guide.*[4]

Discuss with your youth leaders the effectiveness of each program for your particular youth groups.

Ask them to be your eyes and ears on the street as to what kind of programs are needed by the other young people in their neighborhoods and schools.

Discuss ways to involve the youth in being part of the solution and show them how their involvement can help bring change to their neighborhoods and schools.

Retention:

Ask Your Youth Leaders and Parents to:

Listen to what teens are saying all around them.

Compile the types of questions and concerns they hear teens asking.

Bring these questions to your next meeting so you can work together to find the answers.

Come up with suggestions for how to get at the root causes of teen violence in and around their neighborhoods and schools.

Have them read the next chapter before your next meeting.

---

[4] (www.cdc.gov/ violenceprevention/pub/preventingyv.html).

PART II

HOW DO WE COMMUNICATE WITH TODAY'S YOUTH?

Chapter 4

Three Essentials for Communication

While listening to a tape by Greg Johnson, I picked up three words that have meant the difference in my ability to break the ice and actually obtain results while trying to communicate with young people.

Inspiration (Feelings)

The first of these three words was inspiration. Have you ever been in a meeting or tried to listen to someone but were unable to focus on the speaker? The interest just was not there. If the frame of mind is not set to listen, it is difficult to accept instruction. One of the most important things to remember when trying to communicate with young people is to first build rapport. We call this inspiration (feelings). Demanding attention or transmitting information before rapport has been established is nearly impossible. The first five minutes are of utmost importance. An attitude of interest can be developed with a handshake, smile, appearance, or music. It must be accepted that communication is a learned skill. Those who desire to reach youth and change lives can do so through effective

67

communication. At any point in time, everyone brings the same elements to the communication table.

- We bring our bodies, which move and have form and shape.
- We bring our values, those concepts that represent each person's way of trying to survive and live a "good" life (the "oughts" and "shoulds").
- We bring our expectations of the moment, gleaned from past experience.
- We bring our sense organs—eyes, ears, nose, mouth and skin, which enable us to see, hear, smell, taste, touch and be touched.
- We bring our ability to talk—words and voice.
- We bring our brains—the storehouses of our knowledge, what we have learned from past experience, what we have read, and what has been recorded in both hemispheres of our brains. We respond to communication like a video camera. The brain records pictures and sounds in the present.[1]

No matter what your abilities, talent or background, you will find that inspiration, excitement, and feelings must be produced before instruction can be given. This can be accomplished with eye contact, voice inflection, body language, and a positive attitude.

When a principle truth or any other type of message is to be presented, it would serve well to remember that all people love stories. Tell a story from your past and make it alive. Jesus continually told stories as He was teaching. He used the farmer, the fisherman, the birds, the animals and created excitement wherever He went. Jesus' life was one of total excitement.

As relationships with youth are being developed, it is wise to keep in mind that creating an argument is a step in the wrong direction.

The ability to create good communication is not always a result of experience. Some people may conclude that the longer a person teaches, the better they become. Just as ripping through wood dulls the teeth of a carpenter's saw,

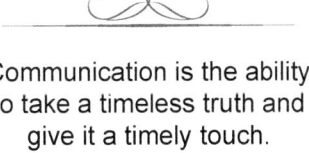

Communication is the ability to take a timeless truth and give it a timely touch.

so experience tends to wear away a once sharp edge. It is important to remember that experience is not the essential ingredient in communication—inspiration is.

One of the best ways to develop excitement is to remember what excites us. Those are the elements that will make others want to listen to you. What touched you when you were a teenager? Maybe it was sports, girls, boys, clothes, cars, horses, school, math—whatever it was, use it! Make a story out of what happened to you. Tell the story of your life, but be excited about it and others will listen. What touched you as a teenager is what will touch other teenagers.

In his book, *Biblical Preaching,* Haddon W. Robinson said there are two important factors in exciting others: "One is what is said and the other is how it is said. Eyes, hands, face, and feet say as much as the words we utter—in fact, more."[2] The idea is to nurture excitement and inspiration before trying to impart information.

Information (Learning)

The second word gleaned from Greg Johnson was "information." There are three keys to effectively informing listeners.

A memorable structure must be produced. This means creating an easy way to remember what is being said. Use an outline that begins each point with the same first word, or perhaps the same first letter. Above all, have a visual structure that makes it easy to remember.

Use humor. This is a must. Use a string of funny stories. Laugh and have fun as you present the message or lesson. Nothing can touch and gain the attention of youth like a sense of humor. The goal is not simply to entertain but to tell a story with the purpose of conveying a message that has meaning and substance. You may need to work on this technique.

In his book, *How to Talk with Teenagers,* G. Wade Rowatt, Jr. had this to say about telling stories to teens:

The art of storytelling with teenagers can be learned; one's storytelling skills can be developed. Granted, some persons are more naturally storytellers than others. Certain personality types communicate through symbol and story while others long for the cold hard facts and give-me-the-bottom-line communication. Even if you, the reader, already communicate fairly well through stories, perhaps a few guidelines will strengthen your storytelling with teenagers. Ask for regular feedback from other adults and teenagers whom you trust as you polish your storytelling techniques. Several tips on telling a story to teenagers are:

- *Know the Audience*

- *Keep the Stories Authentic*

- *Use Active Stories*

- *Keep the Stories Subtle*

- *Use Adventure and Excitement*

- *Use Stories of Humor*[3]

Illustration: an effective communicator will use a potent illustration. Various styles of illustrations are available. It is up to the individual to choose those best suited to the occasion.

Repetition can be boring to teenagers. One teenager was overheard saying, "If I hear one more story on David and Goliath, I think I'll throw up."[4] Try to use other inspirational stories such as those about the victories of Joshua, David, and Moses. The best illustrations are stories that relate to your own personal life and the way the Lord has worked. Most important is that youth are going to pay attention to an illustration from someone they respect and admire. If the life of the speaker is real, youth will be more apt to listen. They respect truism.

Young people are aware of double standards of their teachers. Probably the primary hindrance to youth accepting instruction is their teacher's life not displaying what is being taught. What you are teaching as true must be true in your life if you expect to communicate those principles to young people. Otherwise, they see right through a self-righteous presentation of "do as I say and not as I do."

Greg Johnson related three "C's of Communication" while he was teaching:

Conviction, Confidence, and Christ.

The first "C" is conviction. It is vital that youth see our convictions. Sincerity, enthusiasm, and a deep earnest conviction tears down barriers that allow the real self to break free and have a life of victory.

The second "C" is confidence. When a speaker stands, he should show a sense of confidence that says, "I believe what I am about to tell you." This should be obvious in voice inflection, countenance, and eye contact throughout the presentation. Sincerity in approaching youth, letting them know they are cared for, and exhibiting confidence in the message will produce real communication. Presenting information without action is boring to young people. For students to listen, the speaker should try the action-filled approach. Showing feeling takes action through body language, smiles, laughing, raising and lowering of the voice.

All communication has three essential components: intellect, emotion, and volition—in other words thought, feeling, and action. So whatever it is I want to communicate to another individual, it involves something I know, something I feel, and something I'm doing.

If I know something thoroughly, feel it deeply, and am doing it consistently, I have great potential for being an excellent communicator. In fact, the more thoroughly I know the concept, the more deeply I feel it, and the more consistently I practice, it the greater my potential as a communicator. But all three components must be present.[5]

Emotional action calls for a response from those we are trying to reach with our message. Action must not be confused with emotionalism. Emotionalism tends to be action out of control, without direction or order.

The moment I mention emotions, for example, you may get a little edgy. You think I'm talking about *emotionalism*—but that's emotions out of control, and you ought to fear that. Anything out of control is dangerous. But emotions under control is the name of the game: "God so *loved* the world that he gave..."

The most effective communication always includes an *emotional* ingredient—the *feeling* factor, the excitement element. If I claim to be committed to the eternal truth of the word of God, then it must be reflected in my values, in what I prize, in where I put my time and my money, in what I get excited about.6

The third "C" is Christ. To communicate a message that is going to make a difference in lives, that message must be Christ centered. All that is taught should revolve around the fact that Christ is the answer in life. Through His death, burial, and resurrection, the power of God is available to all that call upon Him.

Instruction (Showing)

While it is important to produce an atmosphere of learning by creating a spirit of enthusiasm (which opens the door for the message to be taken in and absorbed), we now approach a third phase of communication—instruction.

As we examine the three elements of communication—inspiration, information and instruction—it is evident that Jesus Christ illustrates this approach in His ministry.

The key point in instruction is to make the message *believable*. That means the instructor must be believable in action, appearance, and attitude.

The first eight chapters of the gospel of Mark contain numerous illustrations of Jesus speaking to His disciples and showing them through miracles that He is the Son of God.

Jesus drives out evil spirits from a man living in Capernaum (Mark 1:21).

- Jesus heals a paraplegic (Mark 2:1-5).
- Jesus calls followers and appoints them as apostles and challenges them to follow Him (Mark 3:1-19).

After performing these miracles Jesus tells His disciples, "Watch me, do as I do, come and follow me."

Then He taught them the parable of the sower. Mark 4:1-20 contains one of the most foundational lessons in the entire Bible concerning communication for results and retention. Keep in mind when reading the parable of the sower that only souls that were fruitful for the duration were the ones who heard the message, allowed it to find lodging in their soul and take root. Our communication must not only be heard but it must also find lodging in the hearts and souls of our young people. It all begins with giving the message some action with inspiration (excitement).

Jesus continued to teach with this method throughout His ministry:

- He calmed the sea in Mark 4:35.
- Healed a demon-possessed man in Mark 5:6-9.
- Raised a girl from the dead and healed a woman who had been subject to bleeding for twelve years in Mark 5:21-31.
- In Mark 6:30-44 Jesus feeds five thousand people.
- In Mark 7:31-36 He heals a deaf and mute man.
- In Mark 8:1-13 Jesus feeds four thousand people with seven loaves of bread.

Jesus continued showing His power, giving examples of what He could do, often creating great excitement. The disciples finally accept Jesus as the Christ, the Messiah, the One sent of God in Mark 8:29.

The point is, first inspiration and excitement must be created before information can be delivered. Notice that not until Jesus had gained their attention and the disciples had confessed that He was Christ did He give them the real meat of His message. In Mark 8:31, after He had gained the heart of the hearer, He gave them the reason for His coming, the reason for His teaching. The message was ready to be heard. He then began to teach them that the Son of Man must suffer many things and be rejected by the elders, chief priests and teachers of the law, and that He must be killed and, after three days, rise again.

Even after all the preparation for the message, it was difficult for the disciples to accept it. Peter even began to rebuke the Lord.

Jesus continues with the lesson and says, "If you are going to follow me, you must be willing to take up your cross daily." He said to them at this point, "You must be willing to lose your life for my sake that you might save it."

Communication and Retention Action Steps

Preparation:

Begin by asking yourself:

Do I take the time to build rapport before I try to give instruction?

Do I communicate in a personal and positive way?

Am I willing to share personal stories to inspire our leaders and youth?

Have I created an easy way for our youth to remember what is being said?

Do I laugh and have fun as I present the message or lesson at the youth group?

Is what I am teaching true in my own life?

Do I believe what I am teaching?

Read Mark 4:1-20.

Keep in mind when reading the parable of the sower that only souls that were fruitful for the duration were the

ones who heard the message, allowed it to find lodging
in their soul and take root.

Pray and ask the Lord to give you guidance to teach as He did and
communicate His truth so it will lodge in the hearts of your young people.

Communication:

Demonstrate some of the characteristics of an effective youth group:

Greet them at the door by name with a handshake
and a smile.

Have music playing in the background and make eye contact with each one as you shake their hand.

Show them you are glad they are there through your body
language as well as your words.

Tell a story from your past tied into the principle you are
teaching—make it alive, real, and transparent.

Make sure it involves something you know, something
you feel, and something you are doing in your own life.

Make the message *believable* in action, appearance,
and attitude.

Call for a personal response from those you are trying to
reach with your message.

Give them the tools they need to go and do the same.

Remind them this is how Jesus taught His disciples.

Reinforce the concept that we are training our youth to be disciples
of Christ.

Retention:

Challenge them to do what you did, like Jesus did with His disciples.

Give them an assignment that matches up with the principle and story you shared.

If your story talked about praying for a sick person, challenge them to be prepared to pray for a sick friend.

Make sure they know they have the tools they need to do it.

Remind them they are building a testimony to share with their youth group or teens.

Have them journal their experience so they can share it at the next meeting.

Have them read the next chapter before your next meeting.

Chapter 5

The Need to Understand the Present Position of Our Youth Today

We must give attention to the fact that many surveys show evidence that those we are trying to reach do not relate to the mindset of those who were raised in the sixties and seventies, and surely not the fifties. While we want to produce ideal spiritual, dedicated young people, it is important that we understand our today teenagers. Not only do we need to recognize our present generation and their needs, but also understand that within the teenage years, there's a marked difference between middle school students and high school students. One does not reach or teach a middle school student with the techniques and methods that one would use with senior high students.

To be an effective communicator with teenagers, one of the first lessons to be learned is the vast difference between middle school and senior high students. One must be willing to take time to read and study the characteristics and lifestyles of these two groups.

The Real Life of Middle School

Take a look at the middle school student for a moment. Someone has well said, "Junior High [Middle School] ministry is like the story of the cross-eyed discus thrower: he didn't set too many records but he sure kept the crowd awake." Trying to understand the real life middle school student's spiritual growth has all of the comfortable feel of a casual stroll through a mine field. One minute you're speaking to a group of youth that act like they are listening. They are *with* you. The next minute, it is as if you are speaking to a group of unchurched, totally uninterested youth who never knew you.

When ministering to middle school students, it is difficult to tell with which foot one is dealing. At times they walk with one foot in the past as a small child and one foot in the adult world trying to cope with real life.

While speaking at the 1988 Youth Specialties National Youth Workers Convention in Chicago, David Elkind said, "Middle School students should not be required to go to school at all. They should instead be allowed to go somewhere and build a boat."

If they are a building a boat, finding a house for a homeless family, performing a musical, or even playing games, they will learn more about life and values than by sitting in a classroom. Middle School students learn much more by doing than by hearing or reading information. Emphasize experiential spiritual growth activities with Middle School students, and go lightly on the traditional classroom-oriented approach. You will be much more effective!

Teaching Middle school students today brings with it a tremendous challenge as one realizes that the average Middle School student is faced with decisions such as:

79

- *Will I have sex or not?*
- *Will I drink alcohol or not?*
- *Will I use drugs or not?*
- *Will I cheat or not?*
- *Will I believe in God or not?*
- *Will I go to church or not?*

When one considers the media hype, the family structure, school environment, the cultural changes, and realizes the many decisions youth are asked to make, one quickly gets an idea of the help these youth need.

Dr. Victor Strasburger, who is an adolescent medicine specialist, states the following about the adolescent:

Short of being in a war, these are the most dangerous times that adolescents have ever had to face. There are now more choices that teenagers have to make, and less guidance to make those choices. Now, fourteen and fifteen year olds need to decide, am I going to have sex or not? Am I going to smoke pot or not? Am I going to drink or not?[1]

It is unbelievable that our Middle School or middle school students are being faced with such decisions. The fact remains, however, and this is the truth that every Middle School worker must realize and teach with these truths in mind.

The most cost-effective program in any church is a strong Middle School Department. Middle School is now the make-it-or-break-it time for children, in my opinion. Why? Because this is when peer pressures really take hold. Our best efforts and budgeting need to be aimed at doing a good job with youth in this age bracket.

No more important step exists for any church than to develop a highly visible, highly effective Middle School program that will reach significant numbers of boomer youth. Toward that end, an effective starter strategy for your church will be to gather all your Middle School workers together and show them how vital they are, not only in the evangelization of the children, but also to the wider purpose of teaching, through the children, their parents and communities.[2]

Take any two youth workers starting at the same time. Have one invest all his or her time in high school ministry, with the other focusing on Middle School. Each youth ministry grows for the next four years. But, not only will the youth worker focusing on Middle School have a vital ministry, he or she will send waves of youth into a rapidly-growing high school ministry every year. Best of all, most of these incoming students will be the future leaders of the high school ministry, having developed spiritual maturity during their Middle School years. What an incentive to motivate us to pour our lives into the spiritual development of our Middle School student![3]

There seems to be a natural hesitation on the part of many workers not to want to work in Middle School because of what would appear to be the lack of results. In reality, that just isn't so. There are results in Middle School, but you just don't see them many times until after they have been sent to the high school department.

The important focus in this chapter is to learn the traits and characteristics of your age group. Always be aware of the differences between Middle School and senior high students. Both are teenagers, but vastly different in performance and needs.

Middle Schoolers are breaking out of the cocoon and preparing to swim. The Church has the responsibility to see that a Middle Schooler is prepared to fly and knows how to swim. The Middle Schooler will break out of the cocoon and will leave the shallow pool for deeper waters, but they will not survive out of the cocoon unless they can fly. They will drown in deeper waters unless they can swim.

The Real Life of Senior High

It will not be our purpose to develop a discussion on all the various stages of the high school life, but rather to discuss some of the basic characteristics of the high school student. Our aim will be to gain the basic elements that one should look for if he is to be effective in communication.

To begin with, an understanding should be gained of some of the issues that are a part of the high school life. Below is a list of topics that could easily face any high school student on any given day.

- Teenage Rebellion—Why and when?
- The Future—What does it hold?
- Abortion—Should I?
- Christian Service—Can I do it?
- Priorities—What are they?
- Cheating—Is it okay?
- Satanism or the Occult—Is it true?
- Rock and Roll Music—Is it right for me?
- Movies—Which are right or wrong?
- Second Coming of Christ—Is it true?
- AIDS—Could I contract it?
- Parent/Teen Relationship—How can we talk?
- Hard Rock Music—What's the fuss?
- Happiness—How do I find it?
- War—Is it for real?
- Family Life—What is it?
- Boyfriends—Is he for me?
- Girlfriends—Is she for me?
- Dating—What's a good date?

- Parents vs. Peers—Who's opinion?
- Heaven or Hell—Where am I headed?
- Alcohol and Drugs—Should I participate?
- Science vs. Creation—Who's right?
- Responsibility—What is mine?
- Sexual Behavior—Should I?
- Hurt Feelings—How do I cope?
- Hypocrisy—Double standard?
- Lying—Untruth, should I tell it?
- Friends—How do I get them?
- Morality—What is moral and amoral?
- Prayer—Should I?
- Bible—Do I believe it?
- Death—Could it happen to me?
- Pornography—Does it hurt me?
- Church Membership—Do I need it?
- Baptism—Is it for me?
- Homosexuality, Same-Sex Marriage—What is it?
- Faith—Do I have it?
- Jesus—Does He love me?

Adults who communicate with teenagers must understand that each of these subjects needs to be openly discussed. Our youth are living the reality of facing these issues on a daily basis. Becoming acquainted with the complexities of these issues is essential to communication. All youth have concerns that they want to discuss with adults. However, unless we are familiar with these subjects and are well versed, discussion will not be possible. Is your church a safe place for a high school student to ask these questions? Does your church invite inquiry? Are you a "safe person"?

In their book, *Faithful Parents, Faithful Kids,* Greg Johnson and Mike Yorkey state the following in the chapter titled, "Talking With Your Kids":

The communication habits of the families we interviewed was the scariest information we gathered. In a high percentage of Christian homes, parents and children aren't learning to communicate until well after high school or, in many instances, after college!

Only about 20 percent of the adult children stated they communicated well with their parents during the high school years and below. In fact, the teenage years were the worst.

At what age did you communicate worst with your parents? Why? (asked of adult children)

- In high school, because of my attitude and their lack of acceptance."
- "In high school. I was independent and impatient."
- "Whenever I did something they didn't agree with."
- "Middle School through high school were the worst years. I was strong-willed, bossy, and selfish." In high school, because I was tired of deferring to her needs. I felt little respect from her."
- "I never had a problem communicating with my parents, except on the issue of sex. Honestly, I never felt distant from them, probably because I always felt loved, accepted, and trusted."
- "There was never any conflict, but I wasn't as open in high school and college."
- "I was never allowed to be blatantly honest. A lot of denial went on. Any brush with hard truth clamped the communication lid down. That still is happening to some extent today, although there's some improvement."
- "High school was probably the worst. As the oldest child, I felt I was blazing new ground. I know my younger brother and sister

had more freedoms. Our home was never a war zone—just a few battles here and there."

- "When I was a junior, I decided I didn't want to have anything to do with my parents, so I got really involved with activities at church. I decided not to share with them because of my anger toward my dad and his distant attitude."

- "At age eighteen, I thought I was old enough and smart enough to make life-decisions; my parents didn't think so. They were correct."

- "Throughout my teenage years, it was a bit painful because Mom and Dad had a hard time listening—especially Mom. She talks, talks, and talks! I was never given the chance to express my heart because I was a natural listener. I bottled up a lot of things."

- "With my mother, it was in high school. We are both so similar in personality—stubborn, outspoken, and very emotional. It made for some very volatile and lively arguments."[4]

Getting to know teenagers is not as easy as some would have us believe. It is more than just trying to talk like them or trying to dress in a manner that they will accept.

Behavioral and Situational Behavior

There are several behavioral and situational indications one needs to watch for on a daily basis.

Professionals acknowledge that indications of substance abuse are very difficult to evaluate. Parents can observe and identify behavioral changes over a period of time, some of which might be indicators of possible problems. The following is a list of behaviors that may indicate serious problems.

Remember that substance abuse is not necessarily a primary cause.

- Failure to attend class
- Constant use of sunglasses, even indoors
- No eye contact, sullen behavior, extended silence
- Other erratic behaviors

Please be aware that many circumstances and events could cause the behavioral changes mentioned above. **Alcohol/drug usage is only one of the many problems facing children. Some conditions that could cause erratic behavior** are:

- Poor communication with parents, especially of adolescents' opinions and feelings
- Problems with schoolwork
- Lack of "popularity" with peers
- Inability within the family to explain feelings, ideas and beliefs
- Rigid, inflexible and/or over-controlling parenting
- Family move or money problems
- Beginning or end of the school year
- Changes in their bodies
- Parental controversy, conflict or illness
- Parental separation, divorce or remarriage
- Death or disability of a parent

Since some of the above indications are likely to occur within all families, we need to be especially attentive to mood swings and behavioral/physical changes. Alcohol and other drug usage could very well be chosen as a coping mechanism.[5]

I want to mention again that it is not the purpose of this section to deal with the various teenage stages of behavioral actions and solutions, but it is necessary to devote some time discussing the matter of unusual behavioral patterns that may indicate drug or alcohol abuse.

Drugs and Alcohol—Is There a Problem?

The dangers associated with alcohol and drug abuse are dramatic when they touch friend or family, but the actual devastation surrounds us each day in less obvious ways. Who is affected? Consider these facts:

General Statistics

* In the United States, 17.6 million people—about 1 in every 12 adults—abuse alcohol or are alcohol dependent
* The World Health Organization (WHO) reports as of Feb, 2011 that alcohol is to blame for 2.5 million deaths annually
* Alcohol is the leading risk factor in deaths of males aged 15-59
* Relatively few of the more than 17 million US alcohol abusers receive treatment
* Most alcoholics in the US seeking treatment are in the 26-34 age group
* Alcohol dependence and abuse costs the US $220 billion a year
* Over 3 million people in the United States use Cocaine
* More than 10 million people abuse prescription medications in the United States
* As of early 2011, Oxycontin and Xanax have become the 2 most abused prescription drugs
* 9% of high school seniors reported using Cocaine

* 90% of cocaine users smoked, drank, or used marijuana before trying Cocaine

* Nearly half of all drug-related emergency room visits are due to Cocaine abuse

* Nearly 1,000,000 people in the US need treatment for heroin addiction

* Heroin addicts spend between $150 to $200 per day to maintain their addiction

* 1 out of 2 people knows someone who is in recovery from addiction to alcohol and drugs

* Fewer than 20% of Americans say they would think less of someone if they discovered that person is in recovery

Affects of Alcohol/Alcoholism by Age Group

* 25.9% of underage alcohol abusers drink 47.3% of the alcohol consumed by underage drinkers

* A staggering half-a-million US children aged 9 to 12 are addicted to alcohol

* In 2002, 2.6 million binge drinkers were between the ages of 12 and 17

* Alcohol is the drug most frequently used by 12 to 17 year-olds

* Young people who begin drinking before age 15 are four times more likely to develop alcoholism than those who begin drinking at or after age 21

* Of all ethnic groups, Hispanic teens of middle school age are more likely to drink or use marijuana

* One quarter of teens and young adults engage in binge drinking

* Just under 13.8 million US adults have issues with alcohol, and 8.1 million of them officially suffer from alcoholism
* Women are more likely to die of cirrhosis of the liver and violence caused by alcohol abuse, AND die 11 years earlier than their male counterparts
* 3 million US citizens over the age of 60 abuse alcohol or require it to function normally

Family Statistics

* 6.5 million minors in the US live with an alcoholic mother or father
* 40% of alcoholism is passed down through the gene pool
* Approximately 53% of adults in the US have reported that one or more of their close relatives has a drinking problem

Specific Health Issues

* Alcohol is a causal factor in 60 types of diseases and injuries
* Drinking excessively year after year may cause pancreatitis and increases the likelihood of developing cancer of the throat, liver, kidneys, rectum and esophagus
* One out of every five alcoholics who attempt to stop drinking without medical intervention end up dying as a result of alcohol withdrawal delirium
* 68% of those people who come to an emergency room have an alcohol or drug problem
* 20% of suicide victims in the US are alcoholics
* Fetal Alcohol Syndrome is the leading known cause of mental retardation—and the most preventable of all birth defects

* Approximately 50,00 cases of alcohol poisoning are reported each year in the US

* A blood alcohol content (BAC) of 0.5% can cause the heartbeat to be anesthetized and can result in death

Alcohol and Law Enforcement

* More than 40 people die daily from drunk driving, that's approximately 16,000 people a year

* Half a million people were injured in crashes where police reported that alcohol was present. This is an average of one individual injured every two minutes in an alcohol related accident

* 50% of US homicides are alcohol related

* 60% of all people in prison are incarcerated for drug related charges

* 85% of the estimated 2.3 million prison inmates have a serious drug abuse history

* Over 25% prisoners were under the influence of alcohol or drugs when they committed their crimes

* Drugs are involved in a wide range of crimes: Violent 78%, Property 83%, Weapons 77%, and Parole Violations 77%[6]

As we become more aware of the problems of alcohol and drug abuse, the question arises, "What can I do to prevent this from going any further?" A question that should be asked of everyone is, "If I had to communicate with my kids on the issue of drugs and alcohol, how much information could I give them from what I now know about the subject?" The most likely answer to that question is, "Not very much."

The following paragraph outlines why parents must be involved in communicating and helping to prevent alcohol and other drug use.

People often ask me why I think parents are the answer, and I think it is because we have the most to lose. Schools can help, churches can help, law enforcement can help, but no one can replace the family. Being involved with drug and alcohol prevention lets our children know that we care. It strengthens the family and helps us be the kind of parents our children need us to be.[7]

Our children's and grandchildren's lives are at stake as well as our own future happiness, peace, and success. The mixture of young people with drugs is bringing grief, heartache and turmoil to countless families who must then search diligently for answers. Parents' involvement in providing their children all the information available concerning the dangers of alcohol and drug usage is vital.

Again, let us emphasize the importance of learning all we can about the subject and how to use the elements of communication.

Competent Communication

Dr. Edward Courtney, President of Quest for Truth, suggests several good-sense principles for healthy parent/teen communication.

Competent parents concentrate on mastering the basics of communication.

A few good-sense principles guide them:

- Talk less at children and listen more to them. Attentive silence is the simplest way to evoke a child's feelings.
- As important as how we communicate is when we communicate. Become sensitive to a child's prime times to talk. Arrange them or be present when they occur. These precious times are windows to his thoughts.

- Affection is continuous communication. It is love without words. Strong families know the binding power of affection.

- Whenever possible, allow children a voice in family decisions. While in most cases, parents retain the final say, merely being consulted makes a child feel an integral part of the family.

- Stress the importance of education and lifelong learning. It is their future.

- The family home is everyone's home, so make it everyone's responsibility, down to the youngest members.[8]

How Do I Talk With My Children About Alcohol and Drugs?

First, we let them know that we really care about them as persons. If teenagers see that their parents want to be close to them and really do love them, chances are they will open up, share their thoughts and be responsive to what their parents want to teach them. These are the children who probably will not get involved with drugs. The reality of the life today is that drugs are easily available.

Our children are going to have to make a choice whether or not they will use drugs. They will need to possess the courage of their convictions to utilize their resistance skills. But they need our help!

If we have never taken time to talk with our children about alcohol and drugs, perhaps now would be a good time to start. If some of us are uncomfortable talking about these subjects with our children, it's probably because our parents didn't talk with us. When younger children ask about sex or drugs or alcohol, be candid with them. Take time to explain. Be relevant and not too wordy. Answer their questions seriously, frankly and without embarrassment. We, as parents, have to be the most reliable source of information for our children.

If we are going to have any kind of communication with our children, we must be willing to share our real selves with them, not just our ideal selves we would like to have them think we are. We must be brave enough to be open and to relate some of the realities and complexities of our own lives. This is not easy as we begin to rekindle the thoughts, feelings, and experiences we had as youth. If we are successful at rekindling those memories of childhood years, it is possible we can get very uptight with our own children because of possible fears that our children will make the same kinds of mistakes we made during adolescence!

Parents often say, "I can't admit to my teenager the things I did back in high school. This will just set a bad example and give her the right to do the same things I did."

Nothing could be further from the truth. **In fact, your children have known for years that you are not perfect.** Everyone makes mistakes. The key to a family is to have the people who are close to you still love you, warts and all. You build that kind of love when you share your flaws openly with your children. They will not think less of you, on the contrary, they will be much more approachable and willing to listen to what you have to say. All families have their moments of tension and anyone can have his times of imperfection and shortcoming.[9]

Becoming aware of the lifestyles, the vocabulary, and the issues that confront our teenagers is the challenge today for all those who desire to openly communicate and make a difference in their lives. Comprehending the data presented in the last three chapters will give a clearer understanding of the value system and beliefs that are controlling and directing youth nowadays. Building rapport in a family, openly showing affection, and sharing our own life experiences will reveal a caring to young people that will enable them to approach you and be willing to listen to what you have to say.

Communication and Retention Action Steps

Preparation:

Begin by asking yourself:

Have I taken the time to learn the vast difference between middle school and senior high students?

Do I know the characteristics and lifestyles of these two groups?

Am I willing to share my real self with them?

Am I brave enough to relate to some of the realities and complexities of life with our youth?

Have I taken time to gather and share all the information available concerning the dangers of alcohol and drug usage with our youth?

Read *Faithful Parents, Faithful Kids,* Greg Johnson and Mike Yorkey.

Read James 5:13-16.

Pray continually that God would use you in the lives of your local youth and in the leadership training of others who will be doing the same.

Communication:

Becoming aware of the lifestyles, the vocabulary, and the issues that confront our teenagers is the challenge today for all those who desire to openly communicate and make a difference in their lives. Comprehending the data presented in the last three chapters will give a clearer understanding of the value system and beliefs that are controlling and directing youth nowadays.

It is vitally important that we as a church take the time to train our leaders and parents how to build rapport with our young people in our teen groups and in the family.

Start by training your Middle school student leaders and parents.

These children learn much more by doing than by hearing or reading information. Emphasize experiential spiritual growth activities with Middle School students, and go lightly on the traditional classroom-oriented approach.

Realize the average Middle School student is faced with decisions such as:

- *Will I have sex or not?*
- *Will I drink alcohol or not?*
- *Will I use drugs or not?*
- *Will I cheat or not?*
- *Will I believe in God or not?*
- *Will I go to church or not?*

Each of these subjects needs to be openly discussed.

Become acquainted with the complexities of these issues.

All youth have concerns that they want to discuss with adults, but if we are not familiar with these subjects and are not well-versed, discussion will not be possible.

Each leader must ask themselves:

Is our church youth group a safe place for middle and high school students to ask these questions?

Does our church youth group invite inquiry?

Am I a "safe person"?

Parents and leaders need to use this as a check list as they seek to truly communicate with their teens:

- Talk less at children and listen more to them. Attentive silence is the simplest way to evoke a child's feelings.

- As important as how we communicate is when we communicate. Become sensitive to a child's prime times to talk. Arrange them or be present when they occur. These precious times are windows to his thoughts.

- Affection is continuous communication. It is love without words. Strong families know the binding power of affection.

- Whenever possible, allow children a voice in family decisions. While in most cases, parents retain the final say, merely being consulted makes a child feel an integral part of the family.

- Stress the importance of education and lifelong learning. It is their future.

- The family home is everyone's home, so make it everyone's respon-sibility, down to the youngest members.[8]

- When younger children ask about sex or drugs or alcohol, be candid with them.

Retention:

During these training sessions help your leaders and parents learn how to better communicate with middle and high school students with role play and open discussions.

Teach them how to take time to explain issues relevant to their youth.

Demonstrate how to be relevant and not too wordy with explanations.

Show them how to answer their questions seriously, frankly, and without embarrassment.

We, as parents and leaders have to become the most reliable source of information for our children.

Have them read the next chapter before your next meeting.

Chapter 6

The Importance of Role Models

My Dad Had a Way of Teaching

As I look back over the years, I had a wonderful childhood growing up in the small west Texas community of Phillips, Texas. Phillips was the home of the "Fighting Black Hawks" and I went to school with the same buddies from first grade all the way through high school. It was a stabilizing experience. It was a rather unusual community in that all the children's parents worked for the same company, Phillips Petroleum, a large oil and gasoline refinery. Another unusual characteristic of the community was that every house—all 750 of them—looked identical. They had a front porch (about 5'x6'), two bedrooms, a small kitchen, and a back porch (about 8'x10'), some shingles, some windows, and no garage.

Everyone had all things in common as far as the house structure was concerned. It is difficult to remember any peer pressure or comparisons such as "my house versus your house" or "my dad's job versus your dad's job." It was rather nice as I think about it today. I lived on a street that had approximately twenty houses, and there were many, many more streets just like mine. I learned later that our parents leased these homes from Phillips Petroleum Company for $12.50 a month. One of the requirements was that each family had to keep their yards clean and trimmed.

One day I decided to ask my neighbor if I could mow his lawn (back then, we would have said "cut the grass"), and he allowed me to do so. I charged him fifty cents for the front yard and fifty cents for the back yard. That was really pushing it as far as Mr. Cobb was concerned, but he agreed, and I "cut the grass."

I didn't know it at the time, but I was about to learn a lesson in communication that would last a lifetime. In fact to this day, I consider this experience to be one of the greatest expressions of communication a son could ever receive from his father. My dad had a way of teaching back then that should be an example for us today.

Dad Came Home from Work

That evening after I had cut Mr. Cobb's grass, I met my dad as he was walking down our street on the way home from work.

As we made our way toward our house, I said, "Guess what? I mowed Mr. Cobb's grass front and back, and I made a dollar. He gave me fifty cents for the front and fifty cents for the back."

My dad said, "Let me see that dollar."

I reached in my pocket and pulled out my dollar. Dad took the dollar, put it in his pocket and said, "Let's go look at Mr. Cobb's yard."

Without hesitation, we walked over to Mr. Cobb's house, and Dad and I walked around Mr. Cobb's yard, as Dad gave it a close look.

Then he said, "Son, go get your mower, a hoe, and a broom."

When I got back with all the equipment, Dad said something I will never forget.

He said, "Son, let me show you something."

Let Me Show You Something

He said, "See all these little spriggles sticking up?"

The "spriggles" were pieces of Bermuda grass which stuck up about four inches above the rest of the grass. This type of grass was very difficult to cut, especially with the old rotary blade mower I was pushing. These "spriggles" were sticking up all over Mr. Cobb's yard.

Dad said, "Son, let me show you how to cut those little pieces of grass that are sticking up all over this yard."

He began to show me how to do it. He didn't say to me, "Don't you know how to cut this Bermuda grass?" or "Son, you did a lousy job." No, he said, "Let me *show* you something." Taking the mower skillfully in his hands, Dad began to push in short, rhythmic strokes. Then he would back up, and push short, rhythmic strokes. This method actually passed over each strip of grass several times leaving every blade perfectly even.

He then gave me the mower and said, "Let me see you do it."

I began to push the mower in the manner he had demonstrated. I cut Mr. Cobb's entire yard again and this time all the "spriggles" of grass, which made the yard appear so messy were gone.

After I finished with the mowing, my dad said again, "Now, let me *show* you how to edge around the sidewalk. See all that grass growing over the edge and on the sidewalk."

Dad took the hoe and began to dig out the grass next to the sidewalk.

He said, "Do you see what I'm doing?"

"Yes, sir," I said.

"Okay, now you take the hoe and edge both sides of the walk and that portion running up to the porch. Then edge the area around the house and the flower beds, and when you have all that done, rake up all the loose grass and put it in the trash can in the back yard."

After we had finished the cutting, edging, and cleaning up, Dad turned to me and said, "Go get Mr. Cobb and let's ask him if he's satisfied with how the yard looks."

When I asked him what he thought, he said I had done a fine job.

After Dad had shown me how to cut the grass, edge the sidewalks, and clean up, he said, "Now, let me *tell* you something, Son."

Let Me Tell You Something

"Son, I'm proud of you. You took the initiative to ask Mr. Cobb if you could mow his yard for a dollar and that's good, but *let me tell you something*. When you accept the responsibility to do a job, always remember you need to do it right, whether or not you are getting paid. You should do the job the same way you would want someone else to do it for you. Secondly, let me emphasize that you are to complete the job. Finish what you start. Never do a job halfway. Anyone can do that. Do the job the very best way you can, just as I showed you how to do it. Finally, you need to get approval for your work. Do you understand what I am telling you, Son?"

"Yes, sir."

I had learned more than just how to cut the grass. I felt a sense of pride and accomplishment in my work. I have applied these principles to my work all these years since mowing Mr. Cobb's yards. This is an experience I have always cherished.

Let Me Give You Something

After we had completed the job and concluded our conversation, Dad reached into his pocket, pulled out the dollar bill, and said, "Here, take this dollar; do with it whatever you want, but remember that it didn't come easily."

Looking back over that lesson, I have been able to see the wisdom in my dad's instruction and the method he used to motivate me to learn a lesson for a lifetime.

The importance of role models can never be overemphasized. What my dad did for me by *showing* me how to do the job rather than just preaching to me about it made the difference in my ability to receive his message. After modeling the message, he could talk to me in a manner I could understand.

Jesus did this throughout His ministry. Once He said to His disciples, "Stay here and watch with me. I'm going over here on the mountainside to pray. I'll come back in a little while but you watch me and do the same thing here on the mountainside."

While Jesus was continually saying to His disciples, "Watch me and do as I do," the ultimate lesson taught was Jesus giving His life. Even while He was on trial and then placed Himself on the cross, He was saying to His disciples, "Watch me, this is how the surrendered life is lived." He modeled the message He was teaching.

We believe Jesus' method of teaching is the example that should be followed.

As we examine His life, we note there were three stages that He followed.

First, He spent time creating an atmosphere of excitement. With the miracles, signs and wonders, He had something to show them. Jesus also spent a great deal of time saying, "Let me show you something." He taught by example. The key to capturing their attention was showing love, heart, and enthusiasm for the work He was doing to meet their needs.

Second, after gaining their respect and their acceptance by proving His authority, Jesus presented His message. He was the Son of God and He had come to give His life as a ransom to redeem the lost from their sin.

Third, after showing them by example and giving out His message, He told them to go and do the same as He had done. That is where we are today. We have His example before us as we endeavor to communicate it and persuade others to join the family of God. His life and example become the model we are to follow.

By following Jesus' example, we have an opportunity to present a message of faith youth need to hear. The joy and excitement of living the Christian life before our youth is the key to communicating and connecting with them. Only then can we hope to influence them to, "Let Jesus *show them something*" also.

Remember, it was after Jesus had spoken to the stormy sea (Mark 4:35-41), after Jesus healed the demon possessed man (Mark 5:1-13), after Jesus had raised the girl from the dead (Mark 5:21-43), and after Jesus had fed the five thousand with five loaves and two fishes (Mark 6:30-44), that the disciples were willing to accept His authority and confess Jesus as the Christ (Mark 8:27-30). Jesus was in the process of showing them who He was by living His life before them as a life of excitement. It was truly all that He taught.

After presenting and showing His teaching and giving them reason to follow *Him,* Jesus began to teach the real meaning for His coming and the truth of what His life was meant to be. In Mark 8:31-38, Jesus predicts His purpose of life and declares His coming death and victorious resurrection.

After challenging the disciples with His message of the price that would need to be paid, He promised the reward of the coming glory of the Father (Mark 8:38).

When my dad was teaching me how to mow Mr. Cobb's yard, notice that first he said, "Let me show you something, Son." He went through the process himself. It wasn't a matter of his telling me something, but rather showing me by his example.

The most urgent need today in the lives of our youth is adults living as examples before them. Our young people cannot tolerate a double standard. Too many parents and teachers are saying to their youth, "Don't lie. Always tell the truth." When the phone rings, they hear the father say to the mother, "Tell them I'm not here."

We go to church and listen to the pastor preach his heart out, proclaiming the truth, and it happens to hit home, and the message is right on target. But rather than accept the message and do what the Word calls for—repent, surrender, or confess—adults often leave the service without responding. All the while, our youth are watching us, wondering what we are going to do with the truth of the message we have heard.

At this point a critical thought process is going on in the minds of our youth. Their question is, "Is this message speaking to Mom? Is the message going to apply to Dad?" As youth are making decisions regarding their lives, they are watching adults' actions. They conclude that if the church does not work for adults, why should it work for them? They conclude if Jesus' teachings

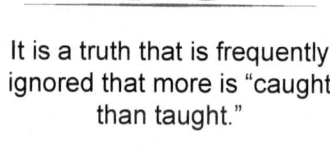

It is a truth that is frequently ignored that more is "caught than taught."

were so important, why don't adults follow them? They conclude, "I don't need the church."

As young people scrutinize the lives of adults they come in contact with daily, they sometimes have to evaluate what they see as a double standard. They are being pulled in two directions—should they follow what adults say or what they do? "People need to see what they ought to be. A cartoon punch line read, "No matter what you teach the child, he insists on behaving like his parents." That's certainly a humbling truth for all parents."[1]

Experts would tell adults who desire to challenge young people that they must realize behavior is learned. Therefore, we must accept the responsibility to teach the right behavior. Our young people's lives tend to reflect our own actions, but at the same time we can continue teaching them.

In his book, *Teaching to Change Lives,* Dr. Howard Hendricks asks the question, "What in the world are we trying to do?" He gave the following outline to answer that question:

Goal Number One: Teach them (students) to think. Whatever you do, be prepared to exploit those teachable moments by helping responsive individuals learn to think. Please note: If you're going to teach them how to think, that presupposes you know how to think yourself.

Goal Number Two: Teach people how to learn. Create learners who will perpetuate the learning process for the rest of their lives.

Goal Number Three: Teach them (students) how to work. Never do for a student what he can do for himself. If you've ever been to Yellowstone National Park, you were probably given a piece of paper by a ranger at the park entrance. On it in big letters was the warning "Do Not Feed the Bears." You no sooner drive into the heart of the park, however, than you see people feeding the bears. When I first saw this I asked a ranger about it.

"Sir," he answered, "you have only a small part of the picture."

He described how the park service personnel in the fall and winter have to carry away the bodies of dead bears—bears who have lost their ability to fend for food.[2]

We desperately need to be teaching our youth today how to think. We must first learn their needs, get to know them, find out where they are coming from, and where they hope to go. Then we must teach them how to make decisions and apply that skill to the choices they face every day. We must impart to them the principles which Jesus taught of the truths that will stabilize their lives, lest they become like the bears and we find their dead bodies lying about waiting for us to pick them up.

Ed Dooley Was Influential

When I was about eight years of age, I visited my grandparents in Tulsa, Oklahoma. It was one of the highlights of my life. In fact the experience of that summer had an effect on my life that brought about a challenge that directed the rest of my life.

While visiting my grandparents, I met one of my mother's five brothers, Ed Dooley. Though he was thirty years older, his personality captivated me. He paid attention to me, played catch with me, taught me how to hold a baseball bat, gave instruction on how to run the bases, took me to the park—he was my friend. I watched as he sang in the choir, and I listened as he read from the Bible. He served in World War II as a bombardier on a B-29 and he was my hero. Through the years, he has been my role model. I wanted to be just like Uncle Ed.

I have not seen Uncle Ed Dooley more than five or six times in the past forty years. But those early years had a great impression on my life. His influence was such that I wanted to pattern my life after his. I doubt if he ever realized what his actions had triggered in a young boy's eyes.

My life as a student, employee, ball player, young man in college, husband, father, and Christian has in many ways been patterned after the example I saw in Uncle Ed Dooley. I cannot tell you why Uncle Ed had such an impact on my life, but I have thought about it through the years, and it occurs to me that modeling is one of the strongest factors in directing the lives of our youth. Ed Dooley had a profound effect on my life. We can have a profound effect on our youth.

Parents and Modeling

One of the more recent studies by the National Institute on Drug Abuse says that forty-one percent of high school seniors got drunk in the last two weeks of high school—consuming five or more drinks in a row. Two-thirds say they have used illegal drugs. Suicides are up three hundred percent in recent years and are now a leading cause of teenage deaths. Young people are crying for help, searching for love, and seeking direction in their lives. Kids are confronted with temptations and challenges far different from the world we knew as teenagers.

Rev. Peter Moore with FOCUS (Fellowship of Christian in Universities and Schools) said:

"The future of the church will rise or fall on our success to communicate deep convictions in the lives of our youth. FOCUS' goal is to help youth ask basic questions in a way they won't be laughed at. The three big ones are God, sex, and death," he said, noting that FOCUS' usual way of answering those questions is either in small fellowship groups or in such exciting settings as a ski weekend at Williams College or at the FOCUS Study Center in Martha's Vineyard, which can house up to 100 students at a time, within a walk of the beach.

The parents who came to the panel at Greenwich Academy, an elegant school on an estate once owned by a Rockefeller, wanted to know how they could communicate better with their own kids.[3]

Connie Lawrence, a psychologist at the University of Bridgeport said, "As teens go from dependence to independence, they must examine all values they have been taught—weigh them and come to their own decision." She cited the Scripture in Proverbs 22:6, but emphasized several key words: "Train a child in the way he should go, and when he is old he will not turn from it." She said the key here is a recognition that it will take time, plus trial and error.

The Prodigal Son had to find out for himself that he was on the wrong path, "Set the teenager free to become his own person. Have faith in God and in him."

Her most important advice, however, was one word: "Listen—especially when you don't agree, listen. Afterwards, you can express your disagreement. The most frequent complaint I hear is 'My parents don't care about me. They don't listen to me.'"

Remember the scripture that declares that parents are given the responsibility to impress their children with the commands of God in Deuteronomy 6:6-7. These verses teach that the parent is going to be held accountable for what they teach their children. So often, the parents leave the teaching of the Scriptures to the church, the Sunday School teacher, or the youth director. We must care enough about our values that we are willing to take the time that is necessary to teach these values and principles to our children.[4]

In his book, *The Key to Your Child's Heart,* Gary Smalley gives a description of four different types of parents.

The first type is the *dominant* parent. These parents tend to produce the most negative qualities in children. Dominant parents have high expectations and offer few rewards when expectations are realized.

A group of psychologists and psychiatrists studied 875 third graders in rural Columbia County, New York, from 1960 to 1981 and made several conclusions concerning dominant parents. They found that high aggression in younger children is caused by the actions of overly dominant parents. This high aggression usually lasts a lifetime and can lead to major violence. The study also showed that harsh punishment, like washing our children's mouths with soap, coupled with rejection can lead to aggressive behavior.

These are some typical statements and actions by dominant parents:

- "Rules are rules. You're late—to bed with no dinner."
- "I won't stand for your back talk. Apologize." (Or slap the child's face.)
- "You don't need reasons. Just do what I say."
- "I don't care how many of your friends will be there. You're not going and I don't want to hear another word about it, do you hear?"
- "No son of mine is going to goof off. You took the job; you get it done."
- "How many times have I told you to stop that? Get in there—you're going to get it!"

These are some possible reactions by children who have dominant parents:

- They rank lowest in self-respect. They have little ability to conform to rules or authority.
- The rigid harshness of the parent breaks the spirit of the child and results in resistance, "clamming up," or rebellion.

- The child usually does not want anything to do with his parents' rules or values. He tends to reject the ideals of his parents.
- The child may be attracted to other children who rebel against their parents and the general rules of society. They may use drugs and participate in other illegal activities.
- The child may be loud and demanding of his rights.
- In a classroom setting, he may cause disruption in order to gain attention from others.[5]

The second type are referred to as *neglectful* parents. He said these parents tend to isolate themselves from their children. Dr. Armand Nicholi, psychiatric professor at Harvard Medical School, states that neglectful parents are not only absent when they are away from home, they rob their children of one of the most important factors in their lives—emotional accessibility. When they are home, they usually are not listening or paying attention to their children.

According to Dr. Nicholi, there are four main reasons why our children are being neglected today:

A. The high divorce rate. Most divorces require single parents to work outside the home, allowing less time for the emotional development of their children. It's very difficult for single parents to provide their children with the necessary time each day for listening and emotional accessibility. However, it's not impossible.

B. The increase of mothers in the work force. The economic pressures of the times also forced many women to seek jobs. By joining the work force, mothers are often less accessible to their children.

Suicide is one evidence of neglect. The CDC in March of 2015 reported that there were 4,600 teen and youth (ages 10-24) suicides annually. There are 575,000 attempts at suicide each year in this age group. 81 percent of those dying from suicide are male.

One study Nicholi's book quoted showed that American parents spend less time with their children than parents in any other nation except England. The study quoted one Russian father who said he would not even think of spending less than two hours daily with his children. In contrast, a study at Boston University found that the average father in the United States spends about thirty-seven seconds a day with his children.

C. Excessive television viewing. This also increased greatly in the sixties and now more than 90 percent of American homes have at least one television. The problem with television is that even though people are physically together in a room, there is very little meaningful and emotional interaction.

D. An increasingly mobile society. About 75% of Americans move every five years (http://www.answers.com/Q/How_often_do_people_move_in_the_US). This robs the child of their parents' time as well as the emotional strength and accessibility they have from friends and relatives in their former home.

Listed below are some typical actions and statements made by neglectful parents:

- "Work it out by yourself. Can't you see I'm busy?"
- "No! I'm expected somewhere else tonight. Get your mother to help you."

- "No, you can't stay up. Remember you wanted to stay up late last night. Stay out of my hair!"
- "That's your problem. I've got to get back to work."
- "Good grief! Can't you kids be more careful?"
- "Late again, for heaven's sake. Would someone please pass the meat?"
- "So you think I'm stupid, huh? Well, that's your problem, buddy. Just get lost."

Here are some possible effects neglectful parents have on their children:

- The harshness and neglect tend to wound the spirit of a child, resulting in rebellion.
- The neglect teaches the child that he is not worth spending time with.
- The child develops insecurity because his parents are never predictable.
- The child may not develop a healthy self-respect because he is not respected and has not learned to control himself.
- Broken promises break the spirit of the child and lower his self-worth.
- The child tends to do poorly in school because he has little motivation.[6]

The third type of parent is the *permissive* parent. Permissive parents tend to be warm, supporting people, but weak in establishing and enforcing rules and limits for their children.

I can look back over my life and see that my parents were of this nature. My mother was so kind and sweet that she could not enforce any rules because she was so loving and protective. My mother had a favorite saying when it came time to give me instruction, correction, or advice. She would say, "Son, have you prayed about that?" or "What do you think Jesus would think about that?" She was such a sweet, godly mother that you could not disobey her to any great degree. She was forever saying, "Well, Son, you pray about it and whatever you think Jesus would have you do will be all right with me." She was great! But because of her permissiveness, there were areas in which I was not as disciplined as I should have been. I was not as good a student as I should have been. I played too much. I was too young to make many decisions on my own. My father was more strict in many areas, but Mother made it possible for me to have my way more than I should have as a young boy and even as a teenager.

The following statements and actions are typical of permissive parents:

- "Well, okay. You can stay up late this time. I know how much you like this program."
- "You're tired, aren't you? A paper route is a tough job; sure, I'll take you around."
- "I hate to see you under all this pressure from school. Why not rest tomorrow? I'll say you're sick."
- "You didn't hear me call you for dinner. Well, that's all right. Sit down. I don't want you eating a cold dinner."
- "Please don't get angry with me. You're making a scene."
- "Jimmy, please try to hurry. Mommy will be late again if we don't start soon."

These are possible reactions by children who have permissive parents:

- A child senses that he is in the driver's seat and can play the parent accordingly.
- A child develops a feeling of insecurity, like leaning against a wall that appears to be firm, but falls over.
- A child may have little self-respect because he has not learned to control himself and master certain personal disciplines.
- A child learns that because standards are not firm, he can manipulate around the rules.[7]

The fourth type of parent is the *loving and firm* parent who usually has clearly defined rules, limits, and standards for living. There is firmness with clearly defined rules like, "You cannot intentionally harm our furniture or anyone else's." But this firmness is combined with loving altitudes and actions such as:

- "You're late again for dinner, Tiger. How can we work this out together?" (Parents spend time working out solutions with the child.)
- "Hey, I wish I could let you stay up later, but we agreed on this time. Remember what you're like the next day if you miss your sleep?"
- "When we both cool off, let's talk about what needs to be done."
- "You're really stuck, aren't you? I'll help you this time. Then let's figure out how you can get it done yourself the next time."
- "You say all the other girls will be there. I'd like to have more information first."
- "Did you do your piano practice? I hate to do this, but we agreed— no dinner before it's finished. We'll keep it warm for you."
- "You may answer the phone, but before you answer, you must learn to answer it the right way."

Typical characteristics of children who have loving and firm parents:

- The warm support and clearly defined limits tend to build self-respect within the child.
- A child is more content when he has learned to control himself.
- His world is more secure when he realizes that there are limits which are unbending, and he understands why—the underlying principles.
- Because the spirit of the child is not closed, the lines of communication are open with parents. There is less chance of the "rebellious teen years."
- The children from loving and firm parents ranked highest in (a) self-respect, (b) capacity to conform to authorities at school, church, etc., (c) greater interest in their parents' faith in God, and (d) greater tendency not to join a rebellious group.[8]

In summarizing parental types, Smalley states that the two most important factors in raising children are: (1) to set well defined, enforceable rules in the home which have an obvious consequence if broken; and (2) to make a conscious, dedicated effort to give each child love and security.

Reaping What We Sow

Galatians 6:7-8 reminds us, "Be not deceived; God is not mocked: for whatsoever a man sows that shall he also reap. For he that sows to his flesh shall of the flesh reap corruption; but he that sows to the Spirit shall of the Spirit reap life everlasting." We must teach our youth that the decisions they make today will follow them into the future. No greater lesson can be imparted to your children than the principle of sowing and reaping.

Children must be allowed to experience the reaping, be it good or bad. For example, if a child spends a lot of time and effort in writing a research paper, then receives a good grade, he has reaped what he sowed. Or a child may go out for a drive, exceed the speed limit and get a ticket. That child has also reaped what he sowed. Living by biblical principles will reap God's blessing in your life. This principle is clear in Josh. 1:8: "This book of the Law shall not depart out of thy mouth; but thou shalt meditate therein day and night, that thou mayest observe to do according to all that is written therein: for then thou shalt make thy way prosperous, and then thou shalt have good success."

Keep in mind as our youth learn from this Book of the Law (The Word of God), it is the essential element needed to influence them in life. The advice in this verse is to meditate on the Word, letting it permeate deep into the heart (truly place it in the innermost thoughts and soul) so that it will produce faith and action that will be pleasing to God. He then promises to make our way prosperous and give us success.

We can no longer give orders, direction, and instruction without providing an example in our own lives. If leaders expect to produce results that will last, they need to show they are meditating in the Word of God, that they are hiding the Word of God in their heart, and are obeying God's Word.

Communicating From the Heart

Teaching with the purpose of changing lives is not from head to head but is from heart to heart. Deuteronomy 6:4-6 states: "Hear O Israel: The Lord our God, the Lord is one.

Love the Lord your God with all your heart and with all your soul and with all your strength. These commandments that I give you today are to be upon your hearts." Heart is referring to the whole being—intellect, emotion, and will.

Communicating from the heart is the process of reaching out. Young people are asking for "heart." They want to see adults model that which is *real* in life. It is the *real* part that they read so well. Quite often adults think they have fooled young people when in reality they have not. They may be unable to tell the adult that they see right through their actions. Howard Hendricks, outstanding communicator, states:

Teaching is causing. Causing what? Causing people to learn. That's the simplest definition available. There's a very essential relationship between teaching and learning. It is the teaching-learning process, notice the hyphen. These words are inseparable. If the learner does not learn, we have not taught.

Teaching is what you do; learning is what your students do. We have preserved that distinction in the English language—we never say, "I learned him," because that's impossible. The student must do the learning; all the teacher can do is teach. The evidence of having learned something from the teacher is that change will take place.[9]

Teaching young people in a manner that will nurture growth and development will enable them to think maturely and can effect change in their actions as well as in their attitude.

The apostle Paul spoke of this change in Romans 8:28: "For those God foreknew He also predestined to be

Effective communication by the teacher and successful learning by the student produce change in the heart, which then affects the mind, the soul (emotions), and the will (spirit).

conformed to the likeness of His Son." The word "conform" speaks of the change that takes place as God teaches us the lessons of life. God molds us, making or breaking our traits, as He wills. Heartfelt communication of God's truth reveals to young people that adults do care, and gives youth the opportunity to change (to be "conformed"), which will give the church the chance to retain our youth for the future.

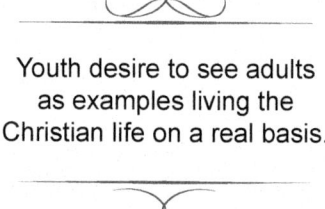

Youth desire to see adults as examples living the Christian life on a real basis.

Their search shines a spotlight on adults they are around every day, and they want to see an example of the realities of Christ in those adults' lives.

Communication and Retention Action Steps

Preparation:

Begin by asking yourself:

Am I conveying a double standard to our young people today?

Am I meditating in the Word of God, hiding the Word of God in my heart, and consistently obeying God's Word?

Am I communicating from head to head or from heart to heart with the young people in my life?

Read Galatians 6:7-8.

Why is there no greater lesson imparted to our children than the principle of sowing and reaping?

Pray that you will be a positive role model for both the young people and the leadership you will be training in your classes.

Communication:

The importance of role models can never be overemphasized. We believe Jesus' method of teaching is the example that should be followed. As we examine His life, we note there were three stages that He followed.

First, He spent time creating an atmosphere of excitement. He taught by example. The key to capturing the people's attention was showing love, heart, and enthusiasm for the work He was doing to meet their needs.

Ask your group to give an example of this.

Second, after gaining their respect and their acceptance by proving His authority, Jesus presented His message.

What was Jesus' message?

Third, He told them to go and do the same as He had done.

Read John 14:12-14.

What acts did Jesus do?

Are there any that we cannot do today? Why?

Read 1 Corinthians 11:1.

Can we say this today?

If not what do we need to do so that we honestly can tell our young people this?

Questions for discussion:

1. What is the most urgent need today in the lives of our youth? (Answer: adults living as examples before them.) Why? (Answer: Our young people cannot tolerate a double standard.)

2. A cartoon punch line read, "No matter what you teach the child, he insists on doing what?" (Answer: Behave like their parents.)

3. Why did the father in the story of the Prodigal Son give the boy his inheritance?

   (The boy had to find out for himself that he was on the wrong path.)

4. What is the most important advice given in this chapter to us as parents and leaders? (Answer: "Listen—especially when you don't agree, listen.)

   Why is this so important? (Answer: It shows we really care about them.)

5. Who is going to be held accountable for what they do or do not teach their children? (Answer: Parents)

   Why is this so important?

(Answer: We must care enough about our values that we are willing to take the time to teach these values and principles to our children.)

In his book, *The Key to Your Child's Heart,* Gary Smalley gives a description of four different types of parents.

Ask you parents and leaders to write the numbers 1-4 on a piece of paper.

As you read the lists of typical statements and actions of each type of parenting style, ask your youth leaders and parents to make a check mark every time they hear one that relates to them next to the appropriate number. (Do not tell them the parenting style you are describing and do not use the same order they are presented in this chapter.)

Ask them to honestly evaluate which best describes their parenting style.

Discuss some alternative ways of responding that would be more productive than those on the dominant, neglectful, and permissive parenting styles.

Retention:

Experts would tell adults who desire to challenge young people that they must realize behavior is learned. Therefore, we must accept the responsibility to teach the right behavior.

Goal Number One: Teach them (students) to _____ (think).
Ask for examples of teachable moments.

Goal Number Two: Teach them how to _____ (learn).
Why is this important?

Goal Number Three: Teach them how to _____ (work).
Why should we never do for a student what he can do for himself?

We must teach them how to make decisions and apply that skill to the choices they face every day.

We must impart to them the principles which Jesus taught of the truths that will stabilize their lives, lest they become like the bears and we find their dead bodies lying about waiting for us to pick them up.

Read the next chapter before our next meeting.

Chapter 7

Lack of Technique:
Which Is Most Important?

———✦✕✦———

question asked frequently is, "Which is more important, the words I say or the life I live?" In communicating with young people, the answer is that both are important. One is equally as important as the other. That question has been asked in an effort to illustrate an answer by asking another question, "Have you ever flown in an airplane?" "Yes." Then let me ask you, "Which is more important, the left wing or the right wing?" The answer obviously is that both are equally important. The same is true of communication with young people. Words AND action to reinforce those words - THAT IS THE NEED.

> What we say must be in harmony with what we do.

Two Musts in Communicating To a Group or Class

When a teacher has the assignment to speak to a group, he/she has been given the responsibility of translating thoughts, actions, and feelings into words and then to effectively communicate that thought with speech.

How many times have you sat through a speech when it was obvious the speaker was unprepared? How many times have you sat through a session when the speaker did not present anything to demand attention? *Preparation* is of paramount importance for effective communication. Knowledge of the subject is vital to communication. During preparation the message can be given form and features. The message needs to be packaged. The ability to package the content is that which separates good communicators from bad ones.

A well-structured introduction is as vital as preparation of the material. The introduction shows knowledge as well as an ability to convey that knowledge. Your preparation should also include a well-developed conclusion. Illustrations can be used to make the lesson apply to the listeners' lives. Once the lesson is in flight, all the groundwork done during preparation will bring it in for a smooth, timely, and safe landing.

If *preparation* is the first wing, then *presentation* is the second wing of that plane. *Presentation* involves voice inflection, eye contact, posture, body language, and gestures. The volume and pitch of the voice can be effectively varied to emphasize important points or to gain attention quickly.

Successful youth communicators will learn early in their experience with young people that the Boy Scout motto applies: "Be prepared."

Teaching Using Different Styles

A wealth of material is available illustrating a wide variety of methods, styles and approaches to communicating with young people. Following is a list of methods that can be adapted and developed to fit your own needs. They are divided into four different categories: *Feeling, Watching and Listening, Thinking,* and *Doing.*

Feeling: Game Show, Pantomime, Write a Rap, Advertisement, Brochure, Advertisement, Brochure, Song Writing, Paraphrase a Hymn, Make Banners, Simulation Games, Collage, Coat of Arms, Murals, Discussion, Posters, Letter Writing, Poetry, Diary/Journal

Watching and Listening: Chalkboard, Maps, Interviews, Overhead Projectors, Video of a Bible Story, Storytelling, Children's Books, Photography, Laser Show, Acrostics, Memory Work, Outlining, Test Taking

Thinking: Agree/Disagree, Debate, Flannel graph, Case Study, Field Trips, Option Play, Questioning, Research, Inductive Study, Tension Getters, Apologetics, Guest Speakers, Leader vs. Student Debates

Doing: Field Trips, Question and Research, Panel Discussion, Dramatization, Role Play, Video of a Bible Study, Game Show, Simulation Games, Video, Let Them Teach Camps and Retreats, Learning Games, Dialogue[1]

One-on-one (I don't want to talk about it)

Parents and teachers undoubtedly have experienced times when troubled, angry or confused teenagers have crossed their paths. All too often adults try to coax them to talk, usually saying something such as, "What's wrong? What's the matter? What's going on? Are you okay?" Similarly, young people may frequently reply, "I don't want to talk about it."

Of course, caring adults want to help, want to be there for them, and want to help solve their problem. How can those caring adults bridge that gap and encourage the teenager to open up and share their feelings and hurts with total freedom and honesty? Conveying your concern, your availability, and your support without being judgmental will hopefully create an atmosphere of acceptance and thus allow communication to occur. Many times just your presence and the fact that you care is more important than the actual words you say. Adults sometimes talk too much! It may be better to *listen* rather than talk.

Communication and Retention Action Steps

Preparation:

Begin by asking yourself:

Is what I say in harmony with what I do?

Do I convey concern and availability to my young person?

Do I talk too much?

Do I need to listen more?

Read James 1:19-20. How can you better implement this principle in your life?

Pray and ask the Lord to show you areas that need to be worked on so you can become a more effective communicator.

Communication:

"Which is more important, the words I say or the life I live?"

(Answer: both are equally important.)

What was the illustration used to ask this question in a different way in this chapter?

("Which is more important, the left wing or the right wing?")

Which method of asking the same question was more effective? Why?

What are the two essentials given is this chapter for effective communication?

(Answer: preparation and presentation)

Discuss what it is like to go to a meeting or a seminar where the teacher/speaker is obviously unprepared.

Discuss what it is like if the teacher/speaker is obviously very prepared.

Discuss the differences.

What does it mean to "package" the knowledge that is to be presented?

Why is the introduction so important?

Retention:

Why is a well-developed conclusion so important in retention of the material presented?

Demonstrate the sandwich method:

Tell them what you are going to discuss.

Present the knowledge you have for them.

Recap what you told them.

As a final wrap up ask for a response of what has been presented.

As you conclude this section, consider breaking into small groups and having each group do a mini presentation using one or a combination of the suggested teaching styles described in this lesson. Depending on the number of people in your group, have some preselected subjects that they draw from a hat, give them a set amount of time to prepare as small teams, and then a set amount of time to present. (For example: Each team has one person give a 5-minute introduction, a second person on the team give a 5-minute presentation of the subject, and a third person give a 5-minute conclusion.)

PART III

WHERE DO WE COMMUNICATE WITH TODAY'S YOUTH?

Chapter 8

Developing Communication and Retention through Family

Family Activity

- "My Dad doesn't really care about church. He goes sometimes, but he doesn't seem like a Christian to me."
- "My mom and dad go to church, but they never talk about it like they are excited. They are always griping about the preacher."
- "Mom and Dad are always fighting and talking about people at the church."
- "My mom says she doesn't have time for church."
- "When my grandmother died, a bunch of people from the church came by and said how sorry they were. That really meant a lot to me."
- "My best friend is Jennifer. She really blew me away the other day. You know what she said to me? She said she was praying for me."

If the preaching and teaching of the Word of God are not supported by positive response, the church service becomes a waste of time. Children "do as we do" but they also "do as we did." It is not unusual for parents to come to Christ at middle-age and find that their child does not share in their decision to follow Christ. The teenager is determined to continue in the path that has been set before them in previous years. The teenager is in a habit of making decisions, especially in the late teens. The challenge for the parent becomes to turn their teenager around even though they have made the same decisions earlier in their own personal lives.

Benjamin Keeley measured the religiosity of both Christian and non-Christian high school students. The results of his study showed that teenagers who recognized their parents as deeply committed to their religion were significantly more religious than teens who saw their parents as less committed.[1]

As a teenager, one of the most impressionable times of my life happened on a Thursday evening about 10:00 P.M. I was late getting home that night. Mother worked an evening job as a cleaning lady for a large office building for Phillips Petroleum Company. I knew my dad would be wondering why I was late. Running into the house, I went into the living room. I looked down the hallway, and toward the door to my parents' bedroom. With only the night light on, I caught a glimpse of the shadow of my Dad kneeling beside his bed praying. I froze in my tracks as I heard him praying for his family and for his only son. It was a moving sight to see this man that had been won to Christ from a life of alcoholism. I have never forgotten that picture.

Through the years I looked back and allowed that scene to be a challenge for the power of God. It emphasized what the Lord can do with the life of a father open to Him. My dad was not a model saint, but he was never hypocritical in his actions either. He worked at turning his life around for the Lord, and he would sometimes fall. But he was always genuine and real as a father and as a man trying to live for the Lord. He was an example of honesty and genuineness. He taught me that trying to do right and failing was far better than not trying at all. I remember my dad used to say, "Son, you have two things that you always want to protect, your name and your word." That was good advice then, and it is good advice today.

In P.T.A. Magazine, Virginia Gibbon said a *good* thing when she said, "No matter how hard we resist the idea, there is no substitute for a parent's moral standards and spiritual values."

Don't Miss These Seven

The family's influence is vital in developing a positive attitude in teenagers about church and religion. Here are seven suggestions parents can use to improve relationships with their teens.

1. **Renew your own passion for Christ.** "Create in me a clean heart, O God, and renew a right spirit within me ... Restore to me the joy of my salvation" (Psalm 51:10, 12). Look for reasons our teens are apathetic about their faith, and we need look no further than our own lifeless rituals and barren religious routines. Teens hear the same church prayers and trite religious clichés and write them off as meaningless.

1. **Verbally express love for your teenager.** In my experience as director of Singing Hills Youth Camp, I observed numerous examples of the lack of love in young lives. I was moved to hear a teen at the end of one day as everyone gathered in a circle for devotions. With tears in her eyes she said, "I cannot remember my mom or dad ever telling me they love me." Ephesians 5:1-2 (NLT) reads, "Imitate God, therefore, in everything you do, because you are his dear children. Live

a life filled with love, following the example of Christ. He loved us* and offered himself as a sacrifice for us, a pleasing aroma to God."

A parent's love is the critical need for teens which cannot be filled by anyone else. The lack of love and discipline in the parent-child relationship is likely to have a detrimental effect on the child's character.

2. **Keep their confidence and take them seriously.** One of the character traits that is essential in developing a strong relationship is the ability to keep a secret. Friendships are made when intimacy is shared and kept within the confines of a special few. Teens are eager to share these special moments if they can trust parents. Wise is the parent who will take seriously this matter considered important by their teen. Privileged is the mother or father who is trusted as a sounding board and confidant.

3. **Be vulnerable, and admit it when you're wrong.** Being vulnerable and confessing your own humanity can have two positive effects upon the relationship with your teen. Showing vulnerability makes you a touchable person. It is almost impossible to feel close to someone who insists on always being right. It was a happy day in my life as a young father when I learned to laugh at myself. Miserable is the one who tries to hide his weaknesses. Be willing to expose weaknesses. Admitting your weaknesses helps your children accept their weaknesses. It also helps them overcome their own anxieties, discouragements, and failures.

4. **Never embarrass your teenager.** Matthew 18:15 says: "... and if thy brother trespass against thee, go and tell him his fault

between thee and him alone..." Demeaning young people by addressing personal problems in front of their friends can be devastating. Parents need time in quiet moments to build trust; they need to be open and available and catch those few teachable opportunities; and confronting issues which cause embarrassment destroys that trust which took so long to build.

5. **Forgive and forget.** 1 Corinthians 13:5 teaches us that love keeps no record of wrongs. One of the most exciting truths in the Word of God is to know that God's forgiveness also involves forgetting. When God forgives sin through heartfelt confession and repentance, He forgives and remembers it no more (Hebrews 8:12). If God can erase all record of sins against Him through His grace, He can lead us to forgive and forget. Giving teens room to fail will pay great dividends in building a relationship. An excellent rule to learn early in your experience as a parent with teenagers is that there are no unforgivable or unforgettable sins.

6. **Give your teenager your time.** "... redeeming the time, for the days are evil..." (Ephesians 5:16). The character of a child is largely formed by the time he leaves elementary school. Nevertheless, we should not presume that our influence or responsibility as parents is diminished. Quite the opposite is true. There are whole new dimensions that evolve when building a relationship with teens. These relationships take time, quality time.

As a parent of two teenagers, I remember it was about an hour's drive to the high school our children attended. Those few years of riding with my son and daughter were cherished times as we had the opportunity to share. Some days there was not much talking, but for two hours a day we were together. Just being together was meaningful. Time is one of the greatest gifts we can give. Setting aside a weekend or a special day means so much. Take your daughter on a date. Take your son to a ball game. Where you go is not as important as taking some special time to spend with them.

Our goal as a parent and a Christian is to make a difference in building the relationships within the family by giving the most valuable thing you have—your time. This gift will have an effect on the family now as well as in the **future** as teens become parents and Christian servants.

The Keys to Your Child's Heart

In his book, *The Keys to Your Child's Heart,* Gary Smalley reveals parents sometimes are not aware that the way they communicate offends their children. He outlines below some of the ways we inhibit our ability to interact with youth:

- Lacking interest in things that are special to me.
- Breaking promises.
- Criticizing unjustly.
- Allowing my brother or sister to put me down.
- Misunderstanding my motives.
- Speaking carelessly.
- Punishing me for something for which I already had been punished.
- Telling me that my opinions don't really matter.
- Giving me the feeling that they never make mistakes.
- Not being gentle when pointing out my weaknesses or blind spots.
- Lecturing me and not understanding when all I need is some support.

- Never telling me "I love you." Never showing me physical affection.
- Not spending time alone with me.
- Being insensitive, rough, and breaking promises.
- Being thoughtless.
- Never telling me "thank you."
- Not spending time together.
- Being insensitive to my trials.
- Speaking harsh words.
- Being inconsistent.
- Being taken for granted.
- Being told how to do something that I was doing on my own.
- Nagging me.
- Bossing me.
- Feeling unnoticed or unappreciated.
- Being ignored.
- Not being considered a thinking and feeling person.
- Being too busy to care for me and listen to me.
- Dismissing my needs as unimportant, especially when their work or hobby is more important.
- Bringing up old mistakes from the past to deal with present problems.
- Teasing excessively.
- Not noticing my accomplishments.
- Making tactless comments.
- Liking me only for my physical looks or abilities, instead of what's inside me.
- Not being praised and appreciated.
- Being built up and then let down.
- Getting my hopes up to do something as a family and then not following through.

- Being corrected without being reminded that they love me.
- Being disciplined in harshness and anger.
- Not reasoning with me, and never giving me an explanation of why I'm being disciplined.
- Misusing brute force.
- Reacting to me in the opposite way I think a Christian should treat me.
- Raising their voices to each other.
- Not being interested in who I am.
- Cutting down something I am doing or someone I am with as being dumb or stupid.
- Using foul language when they are upset with me.
- Being impatient, which often comes across as rudeness.
- Saying "no" without giving a reason.
- Not praising me.
- Sensing a difference between what is said with the mouth and what is said through facial expressions.
- Making sarcastic remarks about me.
- Making fun of my hopes, dreams, and accomplishments.
- Punishing me severely for something I didn't do.
- Being distracted when I really have something to say.
- Insulting me in front of others.
- Speaking before thinking through how it will affect me.
- Pressuring me when I already feel low or offended.
- Comparing me with other youth at school and telling me how wonderful they are and that they wish I could be better.
- Forcing me to argue with them when I'm really hurt inside.
- Being treated like a child.
- Not approving of what I do or how I do it. I keep trying to get their approval but they just won't give it.

- Seeing them do the very things they tell me not to do.
- Ignoring me when I ask for advice because they are too busy.
- Ignoring me and not introducing me to people who come to the house or we see in public.
- Showing favoritism toward my brother or sister.
- Acting as if something I want is of little importance.
- Not feeling like I am special to them. It's so important to me to have my parents let me know, even in small ways, that I'm special to them.
- Seeing the adults put each other down especially in front of company.
- Seldom touching or holding me.
- Hearing the adults bickering at each other to the point where one of them is really hurt.
- Not trusting me.
- Making fun of something physically different about me.
- Seeing the adults at home fighting.
- Sensing that my parent never approves of what I do or how I do it.
- Not being able to control their anger.
- Getting mad at me because I can't keep up their schedules or abilities.
- Making me feel like they wish they never had me in the first place.
- Not having enough time for me.
- Needing my parents but they are glued to the television.
- Seeing my parent spend a lot of money on their pleasures, but when I want something, they don't seem to have the money.
- Making me feel childish.
- Not spending the time to understand what I am trying to say.
- Yelling at me when I already know I'm wrong.
- Making me feel like I hadn't tried to improve at something when I really had

These are suggested areas to examine when you feel that your child is closing up and drawing away from you. It is possible to remove the barrier if you will be honest with yourself. Offering an apology and asking for forgiveness could reestablish communication. It is the responsibility of the parent, teacher, or friend, to look at these possibilities. It could be your fault!

Family Goals

That comic writer and character, Alfred E. Newman, stated, "I really don't know what I want from life but I'm pretty sure it ain't what I've got." There are so many young people today who have not been challenged or given the opportunity to select goals for their lives. One of our primary challenges today is to develop young people with ambition and desire to make their lives count for God and country. It is a great joy in life to be a contributor to society and the lives of others. We must help youth develop vision and goals in their hearts and minds. They need a desire to achieve.

What is a Teenage Goal?

A goal is a fundamental unit of life's architectural design. With the slightest encouragement, any teenager can close their eyes and dream of a whole new life. If that dream is to become reality, however, it will have to be built one piece at a time. This process demands that the steps chosen be in an obvious sequence. Each step can be refined to make it reachable. To help in attaining goals, consider these two basic rules:

Rule Number One: A goal needs to be concrete.

Proverbs 3:5-6 says: "Trust in the Lord with all thine heart; and lean not unto thine own understanding. In all thy ways acknowledge Him and he shall direct thy paths." Psalm 37:4 says: "Delight thyself also in the Lord; and he shall give thee the desires of thine heart."

As one is willing to turn to the Lord and ask for direction and guidance, God says He will give that understanding with direction. He also says He will give one the desires of their heart. What is the desire that God has given you? What is the joy of your heart? It could be that the talent and gifts that God has given you contribute to the goals that should be set.

Parents need to support their teens in the goals they set for their lives. Their goals may not coincide with the goals the parents choose. Each person is born with varying gifts and talents. A teenager may have the goal to do one thing while his parents may have something completely different in mind. Parents could help teens set specific goals, but may need to let them have the experience of seeing the results of setting unrealistic goals. Parents need to support the teenager in their ambition of the moment. It may change, and probably will, but allow them the option as long as it is not harmful.

Setting a target date is part of an effective plan to achieve a goal. Concrete action must then be taken toward the goal. For example, if the goal is to become a medical doctor, you start by enrolling in college. The parents' role in support of their teenager is more than just being encouraging as they attempt to determine which path in life they plan to follow. Many teens do not have direction or concrete goals for their lives. How many teenagers go through adolescence never having been challenged to set goals for life?

Let's examine two elements that give direction in choosing a goal.

Rule Number One: Touchstone.

Touchstone is the core emotional element of the goal. It is the center or heart of that goal. It is the creative part of it all—the fulfillment, the fame, the money, the chance to help people—it is the love of all of it. Teens need to be challenged to describe the touchstone in their own words. The goal needs to be stated in as few words as possible. Every teen is longing for someone to help them reach their goal in the shortest, most meaningful, gratifying route possible.

Finding a role model is the second element in goal setting. Role models have been successful in setting and attaining goals, and they can help clarify goals and be available for mentoring. Parents must realize that teens need inspiration, encouragement, and practical guidance. Teenagers often put pictures of their role models on a desk or wall in their room. It could be revealing to notice whose pictures are on their walls.

Rule Number Two: Set the goal and mean it!

Goals come in different packages, sizes, and shapes. For example they could include making the football team, becoming prom queen, or losing ten pounds. The truth is that most teens' goals can be reached if they are challenged to put them concretely and mean it.

Of course, as one grows and matures, the goals grow and mature. The importance of giving direction and encouragement to young people cannot be overemphasized.

The ultimate goal of every parent should be to encourage young people to be everything they want to be, giving support, and helping them establish goals. It is important to remember that young people need to be allowed to dream. Realizing that the goals are going to change as maturity occurs helps the parent continue to encourage and support over the course of time.

Many parents are guilty of wanting children to fulfill the dreams they had as children instead of allowing the teenager to dream their own.

A common misconception is that once you determine what you want, you must stay with that for life. That is not so. This attitude has become one of the barriers that makes it difficult to take action. Many teenagers hesitate to commit themselves to a particular choice because they are afraid it will be a life sentence. This is not the case, and direction can always be changed.

> Goals do not exist for us to serve them. If a particular goal is not serving its purpose in life, change it.

Goals for the Whole Family

We are all aware that these are difficult times for the traditional family. Observe the media's reporting in favor of alternative lifestyles; the "politically correct" movement that seeks to dismantle the traditional elements of the family; music, movies, and television programs that show families as divided and weak; schools that refuse to or legally cannot teach traditional family views; churches that fail to provide for the practical needs of families; and government policies that penalize traditional families and provide incentives to contemporary family experiments. Is it reasonable to believe that the traditional family will survive? The answer is unequivocally, "Yes!"

There are several reasons why this will be so. Biblical marriage is the best system for protecting and nurturing spouses and children. No alternative has been developed. Many have tried, but none have proven the test of time like the God-ordained plan for a man and a woman to commit to each other for a lifetime. Yes, there are problems that arise and compromises that must be made, but the test of time has proven that the vows of a man and woman committing to each other in the sight of God is the best of all plans. He has not changed His mind about the wisdom of this plan, even though there are always going to be discussions that call for reconciliation and redirection through the course of life. There will always be problems, but that is all part of being human.

Families with traditional values and beliefs need to know that God's way continues to be the most effective means available for giving direction to youth.

George Barna Research noted several characteristics of a strong family. The ingredients common to most strong families appear to include:

o   strong, supportive, honest communication

o   a significant quantity of time spent together

o   shared religious faith and practice

o   agreement on key values

o   love, consideration, understanding, mutual appreciation

o   common interests, goals, and purposes

o   ability to positively negotiate solutions to crises

o   commitment to deepening the intra-family relationships

o   optimism about the stability of the family

o   a firm parental coalition in dealing with children

o   willingness to sacrifice personal interest and resources for the good of the family

o   behavior that earns the trust of family members (for instance, sexual fidelity, financial integrity, and so on)[3]

The above goals may not be easy to achieve, but they are worth striving toward if the result is a functional and healthy family. It is hard work and may require more commitment than other endeavors, but it is attainable.

Considering the hostility that seems to be aimed at the traditional family, it could appear impossible to sustain a lifestyle based on traditional values today. Here are suggested actions which can be taken to achieve strong, growing families.

1. Encourage balance in life. Realize that God has an intended purpose for each individual. He wants His people to have His perspective on life. Balancing our lives is essential.

2. Educate the children while they are in the home. Parents have the responsibility to develop the basic building blocks of life in their children. Parents must take the initiative and educate their children in critical areas of life, using the Bible as the ultimate authority. The family ought to be the place from which a child develops his or her own ideas about materialism, sexuality, relationships, and family and civic responsibilities.

3. Participate in the political process. Parents have a duty and privilege to influence local, state, and federal legislation that will dictate the environment in which a family lives. The only way to protect the freedoms we possess, and to restore some of those that have been removed is to become involved in the political process. Through letters and calls to officials, voting on important issues, attending town meetings, joining advocacy groups, and praying for God's direction in the political process, we can be can **active** participants.

What Keeps Us From Communicating?

Open communication in the home is the urgent need we face in families today. We must be able to talk with youth freely. This is a foundational element in raising children to have a healthy functional life. In their book, *Faithful Parents, Faithful Kids,* Johnson and Yorkey list several *Communication Killers*.[4]

Communication Killer Number One: Not taking time for each other.

The importance of time spent with children cannot be measured. Everyone remembers how much our parents' presence was desired at certain times. One of the most disappointing times of my childhood occurred one evening as I was waiting for my dad to come home so we could go on a trip to the lake. I had looked forward to what we would be doing together that evening. At school that day, all I could talk about was my dad coming home from work and the two of us going fishing that evening. The only problem was, he never showed up! He forgot about the date we had together for the evening.

Time with your youth could well be the most important investment you could make with them. Examine the number of hours spent with your youth and decide if more time would be beneficial in establishing a better relationship. It will probably cost you financially as well as cause you to rearrange your schedule, but it will be worth all your time and money.[5]

Communication Killer Number Two: The thing everyone stares at-a device like television, computer, video games, tablet, or mobile device.

There are things that rob families of their ability to talk, listen, share together, enjoy each other's time, and just plain playing around. Most homes these days have a television for each member of the family. Not always, but generally speaking, there is a television in each bedroom as well as one in the living room and kitchen. Nice touch, I'm sure, but the point is that we are allowing our minds to be filled with the propaganda of whatever our devices or social media wants us to hear and we, as families, are not talking. We are addicted to the noise of it all.

Our devices have taken away our creative ability to communicate with each other. What would happen if we made a rule... no devices from 5:00 PM until 5:00 AM? Would we talk more? Probably. Our devices have, no doubt, robbed our families of the joy of talking and truly learning the needs and hurts of our own family members. We are also ingrained with the world's philosophy of humanism through this medium.[6]

Communication Killer Number Three: Little children growing into obnoxious teenagers.

Little children growing into obnoxious teenagers has become the norm more times than most of us want to admit. Three things are inevitable as youth grow up—puberty, peer pressure, and pop culture.

There are several influences reaching for the attention of our youth. While one is yelling on the inside, one is whispering in his ear, the other is testing his thoughts by what he sees and hears.

Since we can't prevent puberty, protecting them from the next two is tempting, although we know, in reality, that we can't do that, either. Do you really want to shelter them from the realities of life? It is virtually impossible to protect them from all the negatives that this life has to offer. Are we not wise to teach them how to cope with the real life rather than to try to build an artificial one that, in the final analysis, is going to be the real world anyway? No matter what we do for our youth, we are not always going to be able to communicate as we would like to with them. As our youth begin trying to become their own person, they experience that hormone explosion, they tend to close up, and want to be with their friends more than you. All of this tends to cause parents to panic.[7]

Parents do crazy things when their children reach the teenage years. Panic sets in, and they start frantically looking for answers. Sometimes they will move to a smaller city, thinking this is the answer when the smaller town may have less ability to meet their needs. Smaller schools mean less programs and fewer activities to meet the appetite that was created in the larger and more progressive school system. A parent will sometimes change churches, thinking a new youth group will be the answer. In reality they are pulling youth up by the roots and compounding the problem by placing new demands on them. They now have to make new friends, which is an added pressure and is risky because they are open to the first group that comes along. It could be good, but it could also mean they may end up in the wrong crowd. For some this plunge into parenting obnoxious teenagers begins in early Middle School and for some it will be mid-senior high. The important thing is that parents make every effort to be prepared for this change. Do not panic! Keeping communication open in every way possible will become an everyday effort. Your presence and the prayer on your heart makes the difference.

As a young pastor going to make that first hospital call, I did not have much visitation experience. Realizing the importance of the pastor's presence, I always tried to arrive as soon as I heard that one of my members was admitted to the hospital. While visiting a member who was at the point of death, I felt very uncomfortable. I felt the need to perform. I was the pastor and felt that I represented God. I should perform some duty to let everyone know that God knew all about it. While trying to do my part, as uncomfortable as I was, there was an old seasoned chaplain in the room with me. After all the people were gone, the old chaplain put his hand on my shoulder and began to talk to me, trying to encourage me. He said, "You know, Pastor, I have learned through the years that when people are crying out for help and need encouragement, it is not what you say, but rather your presence that makes the difference. You do not have to perform. You just need to be there at their time of need." When he told

me that my presence was more important than my words, a load was lifted from me and hospital calls have been a pleasure, not a burden, ever since.

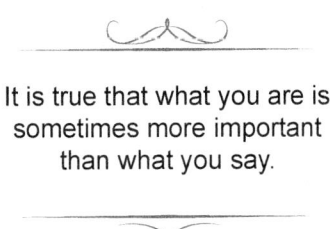

It is true that what you are is sometimes more important than what you say.

Just be there when you are needed. Do not miss that game, that concert, that birthday, that recital. You will be communicating with your kids in a way that words alone cannot express.

Communication Killer Number Four: Not respecting your kids.

One of the most difficult lessons to learn as a parent is to give your child space. We must learn to respect their individuality. Give special attention to their interests. Insensitive is the parent who thinks today that kids "should be seen and not heard," as prior generations did. Today we know that close family ties, open sharing, and supportive actions give children the security they so desperately need. Even though they have only been in the world thirteen years, your teenager is still due your respect.

Communication Killer Number Five: Not inviting them into your world.

As important as it is to be interested in what they are interested in, it is also important that we allow our teenagers to be interested and included in what we are interested in doing with our time. We need to be friends, best friends. Give them your thoughts about a project you are thinking about. Ask their opinion. Consider including them in a major decision

147

you might be making with your job. Give opportunity to share their opinion with the purchase of a new car, or new house, or even a new suit you might buy. Mother, allow your daughter to share in your world of decision making for the family.[8]

Communication Killer Number Six: Not understanding the changes kids go through.

We as parents must learn about the changes that are taking place in our culture. Things are moving ever so fast.

The Major Discipline Issues of the '50s and '60s were:

- Talking in class
- Running in halls
- Chewing Gum
- Leaving Trash in Class
- Not paying attention

Some of the major issues affecting children that make the headlines:

- Alcohol-related traffic accidents
- Abuse of alcohol and other drugs
- Suicide
- Unwanted pregnancy
- Homicide
- Eating disorders (Bulimia and anorexia)
- Depression and boredom
- Sexually transmitted diseases (especially AIDS)
- Gangs, cults and the occult

The contrast is vast, severe and frightening. It has been reported that an average child receives only *14.5 minutes* daily of one-on-one attention from an adult, less than half of those minutes from a parent! Boredom and loneliness for adult company and adult direction put many of our children at risk. *If children rely only on what we parents teach them about the above issues, how much will they know? The answer is usually not very much! The result? Neither the school, nor the church, nor the family has been the primary source of education and training on the crisis issues facing our children.*

So where do our children receive their education and training?

1. Electronic devices—Many spend up to seven hours a day with values being obtained from the media, music, movies, social media, video games, texting, and spending time on their devices instead of with each other.

2. Peer Group—Many teens desire peer or gang approval more than parental approval. One of the teenager's greatest needs is to be accepted, to fit in.[9]

We have the challenge of making ourselves aware of what is taking place in our teenager's world. Only as we are able to understand their world are we able to communicate with them and help them cope with the problems they meet. There are many books that are current and helpful, but more important than the books is keeping our lines of communication open with a willingness to listen and be observant as we pass through our youth's world.[10]

Communication Killer Number Seven: Parental insecurities.

As strange as it may sound, sometimes the parent is more insecure than their own teenager. Sometimes, the parent feels that their teenager has far more education than they do, more talent than they do, or a greater gift to function than they do. This causes insecurity and a parent fails to communicate as they should with their own teenager. Insecure parents don't come down on their youth as they should. They give in too much, and they tend to break down in their abilities to communicate. Parents must take control with faith and courage that God is going to give them direction and strength to do the right things. Secure parents trust their youth. Secure parents raise secure youth. Secure youth can be trusted. When that security is lost, one tends to become a dictator, demanding the unreasonable, and the closeness begins to break down because of feelings of ill trust. Don't allow insecurity to cause doubt regarding the abilities or actions of your youth.[11]

Communication Killer Number Eight: A Know-It-All Parent.

One of the most difficult things a parent will ever do is go to their child and admit that they were wrong. It is difficult, but always insisting that you are right is one of the fastest ways to break down communication with your kids. Using the two simple words, "I'm sorry," will go a long way in melting barriers and keeping the doors of communication open.

Know-it-all parents have to win every time. Robert, a Phoenix man, looks back sadly to a family that couldn't talk because his dad always had to be right. "We never have communicated. On this subject, all of my siblings and I agree: Our family did not communicate—especially serious feelings." Robert says, "My father was a visionary leader, and only his thoughts and feelings were what counted."[12]

Communication Killer Number Nine: Differences in values.

There will always be the process of teaching. Why? As much as we would like our youth to believe something just because we said it, that doesn't always happen. It doesn't happen especially if there are other voices whispering different things... and there are many.[13]

Communication Killer Number Ten: Poor relationship skills.

Improving communication skills will improve your relationship with teens. Our kids deserve the opportunity to talk with parents who have taken the time to learn proper communication habits. Poor relational skills are no excuse. Youth are continually saying that their parents don't listen and don't know what is being said. On the other hand, parents often say that their youth will not listen to them and don't understand what is being said. Much of the misunderstanding could be from the very fact that neither has taken the time to think about relational skills. They are not understood because they are saying things in the wrong manner.[14]

One Sunday evening in December, our Preschool Division was practicing the Christmas drama. The teacher had given out parts to the children. Some were going to be camels, some sheep, some angels, Mary, Joseph, wise men, and shepherds. After the kids were dismissed, I was standing at the door shaking hands and saying good-bye. A five year old grabbed my hand and said, "Preacher, I'm going to be a German Shepherd." The only shepherd he knew of was *his* German Shepherd. He was excited! Misunderstanding can be disastrous.

Communication Killer Number Eleven: Conditional love.

My parents always gave me unconditional love. The one thing I grew up with and never doubted through the teen years was that my mother and dad loved me without restrictions. My mother never put a condition on her affection for me. I knew regardless of what happened, my mother would be there with arms open. My father's love was a tougher kind of love, but it was reassuring to know that they loved me and that was understood. Consequently, I have had difficulty with people who place conditions on their expression of feelings toward me. I am sure you know what I mean. For example, I will buy you a present, but you had better not forget me when my birthday comes. Young people **know** unconditional from conditional.

"Communication Killers" will attack at one time or another in raising your children. The challenge is that you be fair to yourself as a parent. Examine your style. If you detect a "killer" invading your relationship, take the offensive, and be willing to commit yourself to working it out.

Making Time for Family

USA Today (6/15/2009) reported that family time at the end of the first decade of the 21st century decreased some 30% down to eighteen hours a week from twenty-six hours a week due to extensive use of the internet. Much of that is attributed to Facebook and other social media which demands so much time and involvement.[15]

Nearly one-third of all adults claim to be "stressed out" and less than one-fourth of all adults feel they make enough money to live comfortably. Many allow their lives to be driven by the demands of job and other circumstances, leaving little time for family.

Achievement-driven is a lifestyle for the typical American. "I must succeed" is our motto, and to do that we must make every minute count. School gives us a grade that says we have or have not completed the course with a satisfactory level of achievement. Our job description at work gives us a goal that will measure our ability to perform, and our supervisor will give us our report card at the end of the week telling us if our performance measures up.

Even in our casual time, we Americans are driven for performance; such as, setting goals in our golf tournaments with friends, or who's best at tennis, or "yard of the month." If you are one that chooses to really "kick back" and leisurely do nothing on a weekend, you're probably considered to be one that will never be fulfilled and definitely not succeed in life. That's our way of thinking in a success-driven, achieving world. Therefore, our time is spent doing things rather than being a parent to our teens.

Time now is being spent on "How are we going to manage our time." Planning sessions are good. Time well spent is smart time. Adults living in a family household have 168 hours available and spend, on an average, about 56 of those hours sleeping. That leaves 112 hours to make the most of. For the typical adult in a married couple household, employment duties capture the lion's share of the weekly hours. Among the men, roughly 10 of 12 non-sleep hours are spent by working activities. Typically, women spent less job-related hours. But the conclusion is that there are not many hours left in a week to give to the children, spouse, school, church, and activities.

When we observe statistics, it is estimated that of the 168 hours in a week, less than ten hours a week is given directly to the children and spouse.[16]

The Characteristics of a Strong Family

The following characteristics have been suggested as those ingredients that make up a strong, consistent American family.

- strong, supportive, honest communication
- a significant quantity of time spent together
- shared religious faith and practice
- agreement on key values
- love, consideration, understanding, mutual appreciation
- common interests, goals, and purposes
- ability to positively negotiate solutions to crises
- commitment to deepening the intra family relationships
- optimism about the stability of the family
- firm parental coalition in dealing with children
- regular sexual intercourse with the spouse
- willingness to sacrifice personal interests and resources for the good of the family
- behavior that earns the trust of family members (for instance, sexual fidelity, financial integrity, and so on)[17]

It requires a great deal of dedication and hard work for a family to be successful, but it can be done. The result of a cohesive and loving family is one of the most rewarding achievements in life. It is worth all the work.

Encourage Your Family

The American family will only be as strong as you are willing to make it. If you truly want to strengthen your family, the following elements need to be a part of your action plan:

1. Teach your children at home. The training you provide your children is crucial. Society teaches children to achieve, but God wants us to teach our children to be like Him. Teach them that there was meant to be a time for worship (we do that on Sunday) but even more than that we need to teach our children to include Him into every facet of their lives.

2. Train your children to practice Christianity in a realistic way. Train them to use the Bible to search for answers during critical times in their lives. Train them to respect the authority of the Bible for decision making. Home should be the first place a child learns the meaning and principles of life. Schools, clubs and church should be secondary in the learning process. These lessons should be directed from the truth of the word of God.

3. Attend a church that is committed to meeting the needs of the entire family. The church should teach God's plan for the family. That means it should uphold the values of traditional families and warn against the dangers of accepting alternative lifestyles. The Bible clearly spells out God's expectations in caring for the family.

Communication and Retention Action Steps

Preparation:

Begin by asking yourself:

Do I spend more time "telling" and not enough time "showing?"

What characteristics make for a strong family?

How can we better manage our time?

What are your goals for better communications?

Do I show my compassion outwardly and forgive others?

Read: 1 Corinthians 13:4-5, Hebrews 8:12

Pray: Ask the Lord to give you more of a forgiving heart with less criticism of others. Ask the Lord to help you be a better example outwardly and show others with your life how to be a better testimony before others.

Communication:

Discuss the seven suggestions parents can use to improve relationships with their teens.

Ask your parents and leaders to evaluate themselves and offer suggestions as to how they have implemented these principles in their relationships with their teens.

1. **Renew your own passion for Christ.**
    Why are our teens apathetic about their faith?
    What can we do about this?

2. **Verbally express love for your teenager.**
    Do we tell our teens we love them?

3. **Keep their confidence and take them seriously.**

Can we be trusted to keep a secret?

Are we trusted as a sounding board and confidant?

How can we improve in this area?

4. **Be vulnerable, and admit it when you're wrong.**

   Are we willing to expose and admit our weaknesses to help our children accept their weaknesses?

   How can we help them overcome their anxieties, discouragements, and failures by doing this?

5. **Never embarrass your teenager.**

   Do we demean young people by addressing personal problems in front of their friends?

   How can we do a better job of addressing these issues with our teens?

6. **Forgive and forget.**

   Do we give our teens room to fail?

   Have we communicated that there are no unforgivable or unforgettable sins?

7. **Give your teenager your time.**

   Are we taking the time to build a relationship with our teens?

   What are some ways we can do this?

Remember: Our goal as a parent, leader, and a Christian is to make a difference in building the relationships within our teens by giving the most valuable thing you have—your time. This gift will have an effect on the families now as well as in the **future** as teens become parents and Christian servants.

One of our primary challenges today is to develop young people with ambition and desire to make their lives count for God and country.

Teens need to be challenged to set a goal for their lives.

Have your parents and leaders describe their own personal goals in as few words as possible.

Use a white board or flip chart to list the ideas you come up with as a group in each of these areas:

Encourage balance in life.

Educate the children in critical areas of life, using the Bible as the ultimate authority about materialism, sexuality, relationships, and family and civic responsibilities.

Participate actively in the political process.

"Communication Killers" will attack at one time or another. Review the list and ask your group if they found one or more "killers" invading their relationship as they read this chapter.

Ask them to share what they did to take the offensive and begin working it out.

Communication Killer Number One: Too busy to take time for each other.

Communication Killer Number Two: Allowing devices to take the place of time together.

Communication Killer Number Three: Panic over obnoxious teenagers.

Communication Killer Number Four: Not respecting your kids.

Communication Killer Number Five: Not inviting them into your world.

Communication Killer Number Six: Not understanding the changes kids go through.

Communication Killer Number Seven: Parental insecurities.

Communication Killer Number Eight: A Know-It-All Parent.

Communication Killer Number Nine: Differences in values.

Communication Killer Number Ten: Poor relationship skills.

Communication Killer Number Eleven: Conditional love.

Retention:

The American family will only be as strong as you are willing to make it.

Teach your children the principles they need to become productive adults by spending time discussing and modeling.

Teach our children to include God in every facet of their lives by example.

Attend a church that is committed to meeting the needs of the entire family and discuss with your children what they have learned.

Chapter 9

Developing Communication and Retention through Church

Fishing with Brother Faulkenberry

*L*ooking back over my life, as a young man brought up in church, I can say that it was in church where I learned the spiritual principles that have guided my life and provided those basic foundational blocks which provide real faith. More can be learned at church than just what is gleaned from the sermon preached.

One of the first challenges that I accepted as a young boy was given by my Sunday School teacher, Brother Faulkenberry. There were about seven boys in his class. He had a difficult time getting us to listen and pay attention while he taught his thirty-minute lesson every Sunday morning. One Sunday he made an announcement. He was going to give a free fishing trip and a brand new rod and reel to the boy that was the best-behaved, brought the most visitors, and read his lesson the most consistently over a six-week period. This was my first challenge that I can recall where I had a chance to do something on my own and win a prize.

I won that contest! Brother Faulkenberry took three other boys and me on an overnight fishing trip. He gave me the rod and reel, along with a big hug. That experience gave a young boy an experience that has been profitable throughout his life. It was my first win. It taught me that I could compete, that I was able to set a goal, and that I was capable of reaching that goal. The thrill of that accomplishment was the source of encouragement that fueled the beginning of expectation. Church is where these relationships become reality. Bro. Faulkenberry was faithful to his promise and his friendship developed my confidence. Brother Faulkenberry, as we all called him, continued to teach those same boys for several years. He gave us memory verses, reading assignments, and always rewarded our good work. To this day, I can say that going to Brother Faulkenberry's class was a deep experience in my life.

Praying Is Talking to God

Youth groups come and go, but as a teenager I attended an exceptional group for young people. There were several of us who had entered the ministry. To this day, we are all still involved in full-time ministry to some degree.

One Sunday evening, I had just been promoted to the Middle School program, and there were about ten of us in the Sunday evening class. The teacher was presenting a lesson on prayer.

She was doing quite well when, all at once, she stopped teaching and asked, "What does it mean to pray?"

She looked at me and said, "What is prayer anyway, John?"

About half shocked, I said, "It's talking to God."

"Exactly right," she said.

After she finished teaching the class, she called on me to pray.

In doing so, she said, "John, will you talk to God for us?"

It was through her lesson and her calling on me to pray that I was encouraged because I could talk to God. After class she gave me a big hug and told me how proud she was of me and how well I had prayed. I always believed that God heard me when I prayed.

I Watched My Parents Listen

An interesting thought has occurred to me as I look back over the years of church- going and especially now as a parent myself. I remember going to church and hearing the pastor preach. As he was preaching, I was asking myself as I watched my parents, "Are they hearing what he is saying?" It is important that we realize our youth are **watching** us **hear** the message. They are wondering what we are going to do with it.

The Bible comes alive when parents receive the message and apply it in their own lives. I will never forget hearing my pastor preach about answered prayer. One evening my dad was at work, and Mother and I were home alone. It began to rain; thunder rolled, lightning flashed across the sky, and hail pelted the house. Mother took me by the hand and said, "Let's pray that the Lord will cause this storm to pass over." We knelt down beside the bed and Mother began to pray. Within thirty seconds, the storm was gone! I mean gone, out of sight, no rain, no thunder, no lightning. I believe God answered her prayer. I never doubted my mother's belief in God after the experience of God answering her prayer. These are the types of lessons that cause biblical retention in the lives of our youth.

Youth need to see that God is real in their parents' lives, and that parents truly care.

Can the Church Help?

The church is the only institution left in our society that consistently speaks out for family values. It can and should speak with confidence and assurance that we need the traditional family. The church can enhance the growth of teenagers and keep them interested and excited about the truth of God's Word through programs geared to their level. Consider the possibility of using some of the following methods for encouraging young people, reaching into the community, and serving the needs of families.

- sponsoring programs that educate young people about family matters, including God's view on sexuality
- developing systems through which teenagers who become pregnant can be assured of a good home for a child if they do not want to raise it, thus reducing the likelihood of abortion
- providing healthy and uplifting entertainment and activities for young people to counter the disturbing ideas pushed at them in the media
- offering adults tangible models of what healthy families look like and of the commitment it takes to maintain a godly family
- providing strong, Biblical teaching on God's intentions for the family, the role of the church in supporting families, and how God tells us to deal with family difficulties and crises
- installing pastors, church staff, and lay leaders only if they have healthy, strong family lives (in fact, the apostle Paul in I Timothy includes this standard as one of the important qualifications for church leaders)
- publicly, forcefully, and intelligently addressing erroneous ideas that have gained wide currency—such as the notion that

cohabitation serves as an insurance policy against divorce, the belief that half of all marriages end in divorce, the 10 percent myth regarding homosexuality, the belief that children rebound from divorce better than adults, and so on

- offering homemakers options that will enable them to use their talents for productive, in-home enterprises that eliminate the need to work outside the home

- developing financial and employment assistance for church families going through difficult times

- supporting adults so strongly that when a marriage is endangered, the church becomes a primary support system, providing encouragement, counseling, prayer support, and the other forms of assistance needed to protect the family

- supporting adults and children from broken families so that they may rebuild their lives in an environment of love and understanding, rather than in isolation, condemnation, and poverty

- adequately motivating and educating Christians, who can in turn influence the political leaders who draft and vote on family policy.[1]

In order to develop young people through the church, a dedicated effort must be made in order to make a difference. If we are serious about reaching teenagers through the churches and truly want our churches to be places of love, understanding, support, and assistance, we must convert our congregations into activist organizations that commit massive resources to serving families and their kids.

A key element in communicating and retaining our youth is the establishment of biblical principles in their hearts and minds that the church was established by God and He has given it the purpose of proclaiming His truth.

Communication and Retention Action Steps

Preparation:

Begin by asking yourself:

Are the youth in my sphere of influence seeing that God is real in my life?

Do they perceive that I truly care about what they are dealing with in their lives?

Read 2 Timothy 3:16

Pray

Communication:

The church is the only institution left in our society that consistently speaks out for family values. We need to make sure we are doing our part.

Ask the members of your group to look up and read each of these scriptures.

Deuteronomy 4:9 – Ask: What are we to teach our children?

Deuteronomy 11:19-22 – Ask: What are we to teach our children?

Deuteronomy 11:26-28 – Ask: Have we seen this principle active today?

> Example: Removing Ten Commandments from schools.
> What are the results of this in our society today?

Titus 2:1, 6-8 – Ask: What are we to teach our young people?

> How are we to accomplish this?

James 3:1, 9-10 – Ask: Why do we need to be careful what we say and teach especially to our young people?

1 Timothy 4:1-3, 6 – Ask: What did the Spirit say was going to happen in these end times?

Are we seeing these things happening in our young people?

If we point these things out what does the Bible say we will be?

1 Timothy 4:8 – Ask: What has value for this present life and the life to come in our lives and in the lives of our youth?

1 Timothy 4:9-12 – Ask: What is the trustworthy saying?

In what ways are we to set an example for our young people?

1 Timothy 4:13-16 – Ask: What are the things listed in this passage that we are to do?

Devote ourselves to _____

Not neglect our _____

Let everyone see _____

Watch closely our _____

Persevere because _____

How important is it to God that we teach our next generation biblical principles?

Discuss the possibility of using some of the following methods for encouraging young people, teaching them godliness, reaching into the community, and serving the needs of families.

- sponsoring programs that educate young people about family matters, including God's view on sexuality

- developing systems through which teenagers who become pregnant can be assured of a good home for a child if they do not want to raise it, thus reducing the likelihood of abortion

- providing healthy and uplifting entertainment and activities for young people to counter the disturbing ideas pushed at them in the media

- offering adults tangible models of what healthy families look like and of the commitment it takes to maintain a godly family

- providing strong, Biblical teaching on God's intentions for the family, the role of the church in supporting families, and how God tells us to deal with family difficulties and crises

- installing pastors, church staff, and lay leaders only if they have healthy, strong family lives (in fact, the apostle Paul in I Timothy includes this standard as one of the important qualifications for church leaders)

- publicly, forcefully, and intelligently addressing erroneous ideas that have gained wide currency—such as the notion that cohabitation serves as an insurance policy against divorce, the belief that half of all marriages end in divorce, the 10 percent myth regarding homosexuality, the belief that children rebound from divorce better than adults, and so on

- offering homemakers options that will enable them to use their talents for productive, in-home enterprises that eliminate the need to work outside the home

- developing financial and employment assistance for church families going through difficult times

- supporting adults so strongly that when a marriage is endangered, the church becomes a primary support system, providing encouragement, counseling, prayer support, and the other forms of assistance needed to protect the family

- supporting adults and children from broken families so that they may rebuild their lives in an environment of love and understanding, rather than in isolation, condemnation, and poverty

Adequately motivating and educating young Christians, who can in turn influence the political leaders who draft and vote on family policy is an essential part of our job description from God.[1]

Retention:

In order to develop young people through the church, a dedicated effort must be made in order to make a difference. If we are serious about reaching teenagers through the churches and truly want our churches to be places of love, understanding, support, and assistance, we must convert our congregations into activist organizations that commit massive resources to serving families and their kids.

Chapter 10

Developing Communication and Retention through School

$\mathcal{M}$any of my life's lessons were communicated to me while I was attending Phillips Elementary and High School in Phillips, Texas (located in the upper Panhandle of Texas). Principals, teachers, and coaches in those schools had a great impact on my life.

Granted, public schools are far different than they were in my years of attending school; however, as recently as this morning, I was the guest speaker in a Middle School just across the street from our church. I read the Bible, prayed, had a question and answer time, a time for prayer requests, and then a closing prayer. Not every school has that privilege, but a few good principals, teachers, and coaches still exist.

In the School

Gary Bauer gives the following observation in his book, *Our Journey Home:*

We know from history that all good educational systems since the time of the Roman Empire have taught the rising generation loyalty to parents and family, a sense of responsibility to the public order, a feeling of duty toward the community, a high regard for human life, respect for nature, and love of beauty and truth. A modern catalog of desired virtues that parents and teachers could agree on would be quite similar.

At a recent conference on education, Professor Christian Hoff Summers of Clark University was pressed to identify some clear issues of right and wrong by academicians who clearly felt that no such things exist. She replied:

"It is wrong to betray a friend, to mistreat a child, to humiliate someone, to torment an animal, to think only of yourself, to lie, to steal, to break promises. And on the positive side, it is right to be considerate and respectful of others, to be charitable, honest and forthright."

She met with a very skeptical reaction.

Of course exceptions can be found to rules such as these. The problem with modern approaches to teaching values is that they mistake the exception for the rule. A typical model problem that advocates of values clarification use on children is: What do you do if you have no money and your mother is dying of starvation? Is it all right to steal? Another common example is to ask children whom they would throw overboard if they were in a lifeboat with six people and could only stay afloat with five. These are interesting mind-bending dilemmas, but the vast majority of life's situations do not involve starving mothers and sinking lifeboats. They involve mundane things such as learning how to live in a family, showing up on time for work, displaying courtesy to fellow citizens, and discharging responsibilities to the community and country. For these tasks, fairly simple rules should suffice.

Moral education is not the same thing as religious education. Teachers in public school classrooms are not permitted to teach theology; that will have to be done in each of our homes. But constitutional prohibitions on promoting sectarian religious beliefs in our schools should not be used as an excuse to avoid teaching about the role of religion in our history and culture. Professor Paul Vitz in a Department of Education study documented a shocking bias against religion in textbooks commonly used in our schools. The Pilgrims, for example, are identified as "people who make long trips" and Christmas as "a warm time for special foods." Not only is this a form of censorship, but it severely damages our children's moral development because so many of the values Americans can agree on have as their source the Judeo-Christian ethic.

Here, for example, is a lesson from McGuffey's first reader, a very popular textbook in public schools until quite recently. "Always do to other children as you wish them to do to you. This is the Golden Rule. So remember it when you play. Act upon it now, and when you are grown up, do not forget it." Suspicious lawyers for the American Civil Liberties Union might detect that this sounds alarmingly like something Christ once said. But what if it is? To teach about the values of the Jewish and Christian religions (as distinct from the doctrine) is to teach love, dignity, forgiveness, courage, candor, and self-sacrifice, all the highest manifestations of what it means to be alive and to be human.

The McGuffey readers were a product of William Holmes McGuffey, an outstanding nineteenth-century educator and preacher. Millions of copies were sold and widely used in American schools. Because of a renewed interest in these classic books, they are now available again through Mott Media, Inc. The seven-volume set is a treasure trove of literary selections—essays, poems, and excerpts from famous speeches by American statesmen.

Just reading the index of the fourth reader gives you a feel for the books. Included in the selections are "Washington's Birthday," "The Field of Waterloo," "The Best Classics," "Happy Consequences of American

Independence," "Prince Arthur," "Anthony's Oration over Caesar," "William Tell," and dozens of other exciting writings for young people.

In our effort to identify values that can be taught in public schools, we should attempt to discover a common body of ethical knowledge that, even if it has a religious origin, serves the purpose of maintaining and strengthening devotion to our country, to democratic institutions, to fellow citizens, to family members, and finally to an ideal of human dignity.[1]

We are continually challenged to make every effort possible to be a witness and a source of encouragement for our youth as they confront the responsibility of getting an education. The process of discipline and the never-ending duty of doing right remains a source of character building in the lives of our young people. Let's be a part and accept our role of support as these youth are willing to building their lives around Christ.

Unattended Marketplace

On public radio I recently heard a report from an astonished businessman who had just returned from Japan and thought he saw fairly clearly why that country was pulling ahead of us competitively. He had been in Osaka, a large Japanese city, and had come across an open-air market that was left completely unattended for more than fifteen minutes. During that time hundreds of shoppers milled around, but not one item was stolen. There was a time when the same thing would have routinely happened in America. It still does in some small communities. But today, can anyone imagine leaving anything of value unguarded for even a moment in New York, Los Angeles, or even in the nation's capital and returning to find it untouched?

Motivational speaker and best seller author Zig Ziglar makes the same observation: "In Japan, starting in kindergarten, one hour a day, every day, until they graduate from high school, they have a course that teaches students the importance of honesty, positive mental attitude, motivation, responsibility, free enterprise, thrift, respect for authority, patriotism, basic values. That's the reason they are eating our lunch in the market place."

What is the bottom line? Schools need to do a better job teaching values, and churches have a role, too. But the Mass Mutual respondents were nearly unanimous (95 percent) in agreeing that the home is the place where the most basic values are either instilled or not. Knowing that should arm everyone, government official included, with a new sense of where to locate the ethics-building activities of the future. Full disclosure and term limitations will remain viable policy weapons, but a society that wants a strong ethical foundation in its leaders will find new ways to shore up Mom and Dad's clear yes and no.[2]

Even though there are many problems in America with crime, drugs and families falling apart, we still have the greatest country in the world. We have allowed some of our basic principles to shift, but America has the opportunity to educate and redevelop these basic biblical principles if we will but turn to the Lord and communicate these truths that we know to be absolute. We have the talent and resources available to communicate. Never has the need been greater for education to rise to the occasion to bring out the best in our students.

We need to build strong ethical foundations in our youth which are derived from the truth of the Word of God and that in turn will produce the character that gives strong beliefs and correct action.

Our churches have a role to play as well as our schools and families. All of us working together with the power of God will make a difference in our communities.

Communication and Retention Action Steps

Preparation:

Begin by asking yourself:

Am I personally involved in my local schools in an effort to help insure what our children are being taught conforms to biblical principles?

Am I involved in the Parent Teacher's organization?

Am I trusting the government to educate our youth?

Am I abdicating my responsibility to instill God's character principles in our young people?

Read James 1:22-25.

Do you read, listen to and study the Word of God and then do something with the truth you have received from it?

Pray and ask God to give you the wisdom to take all that He has given you and use it to equip the next generation to also rightly handle His Word and be doers of the Word as well.

Communication:

We need to build strong ethical foundations in our youth which are derived from the truth of the Word of God and that in turn will produce the character that gives strong beliefs and correct action.

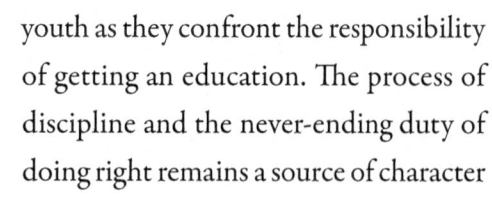

We are continually challenged to make every effort possible to be a witness and a source of encouragement for our youth as they confront the responsibility of getting an education. The process of discipline and the never-ending duty of doing right remains a source of character building in the lives of our young people.

Let's be a part and accept our role of support as these youth are willing to build their lives around Christ.

Our churches have a role to play as well as our schools and families. All of us working together with the power of God will make a difference in our communities.

It is important to know what is being taught in our schools.

Interacting with teachers and school officials, attending school meetings, and becoming aware of the curriculum is very important in making sure the character, moral, and ethic schooling our children receive is godly.

Come up with creative ways to incorporate godly instruction into what your children are learning in school.

Be actively involved in their homework or discussions about what they are being taught.

Work together as parents to stay informed and come up with ways to help youth leaders in the church present relevant issues during youth meetings.

To do this, parents and youth leaders must be taught God's truth and how to present it in a relevant way.

Instruct parents on how to use a concordance, Bible dictionary, and how to research current issues and subjects that are being taught in the local schools.

Each meeting ask your group what needs to be discussed the following week so that parents and youth leaders can coordinate teaching to better equip our youth to deal with social and academic issues.

Retention:

It is time to become doers of the Word.

Ask parents and leaders to do their own research as to what is being taught to their youth.

Each should do a study in God's Word to discover a truth that they can present to their youth and then share with the other parents and leaders at the next meeting.

Ask them to read the next chapter before your next meeting.

Chapter 11

Developing Communication and Retention Through Friends

What is a Friend?

The Word of God tells us, "A man that hath friends must show himself friendly..." (Proverbs 18:24a). How many friends do you have in your life?

Years ago while I was attending a class, the teacher gave an assignment to write a definition of the word **friend.** As I pondered that question, "What is a friend?" I must admit that I was puzzled and hard pressed to find words to put on paper.

My answer was this: A friend is someone you can think out loud to. I am not sure if I heard that definition or read it in the assigned reading. As I verbalized that definition, it began to permeate my thinking and became very meaningful in my life.

How many people can you think out loud to? There are those whom I have trusted and with whom I have shared thoughts only to find out they were not really true friends. Think of those with whom you can share and trust with the thoughts of your heart (thoughts you struggle with that no one else knows). When you need that kind of friend to share these innermost thoughts with, you will find they are few and far between. The Scripture says, "A man of many companions may come to ruin, but there is a friend who sticks closer than a brother" (Proverbs 18:24b NIV). That friend is Jesus.

There are some I would call my friends, but I wonder if they can handle my faults and my mistakes. If they really knew me, really knew my thoughts, would they remain my friends?

It is through our friendships that we gain some of our most needed strength. From them we gain courage to keep moving forward. Through special friends, we obtain needed affirmation. Because of friends, we take courage to tackle the hardest of challenges. Because of friends we gain the wisdom to venture into the unknown. With their help we accomplish life's impossible dreams.

Unmeasured Devotion

The Tompkins family, mother and father and two teenage sons, lived in a trailer park in Woodbridge, Virginia, a southern suburb of Washington. Last April 9, a fire broke out in the trailer while the family was asleep. Their home was quickly engulfed in flames, but the parents managed to scramble outside. Firemen had already arrived and were trying to rescue the boys, Adam and Benjamin, who were trapped in their room. Neighbors tried to restrain Mrs. Tompkins, but she screamed, "My babies are in there," and rushed into the burning trailer.

One spectator remarked, "She was on fire the moment she went through that door." After the blaze was extinguished, firemen found her body just outside the room where Adam and Benjamin lay dead. This age of ours doesn't value folk wisdom very highly, but it was folk wisdom that one of the Tompkins' neighbors relied upon when asked to comment by reporters. "I have heard it said," he replied, "that a mother will go through fire for her children, and that's what she did."

It should give us pause to realize that if we were to go by statistics alone, neighborhoods like the Tompkins' trailer park wouldn't count for much. It would rate low on the income scale and probably very high in dysfunctional families. The experts tell us that abuse and neglect of children are common among the poor. This was probably a neighborhood crawling with social workers checking up on parents. Yet this neighborhood gave us Lillie Tompkins, who shouted, "My babies are in there!" and then rushed with them into the arms of a loving God.

Would any of us not do the same? I don't know when I first realized that the lives of my children and Carol became more important than my own. But I know without a doubt that, like most parents, I would willingly die for my family. Just as importantly, we must live for them.[1]

There are several that I could call my friends, but only eternity will declare the unrevealed truth of this subject, although there are those about whom I will always wonder.

My Family Members are my Best Friends

Susan has been my closest and best friend through the years, even more so than my children. I say that only because my children have not had the opportunity to know life as their mother and I have experienced it. Susan has been my

You have to know that my best friends are my family—my children and my wife.

courage, my strength, and my joy along with the Lord. Susan is one I can think out loud to; she knows my thoughts and understands my weaknesses.

She remains my best friend through our years of marriage. It is wonderful to have family and friends to help you grow in the Lord and encourage you through life's trials. Friends are a source of strength and a blessing from the Lord. There is no greater reward than to have your children rise up and call you blessed. Our children have been a source of joy and strength to Susan and me throughout their lives. We praise the Lord for their love and loyalty to the Lord as well as to their parents. Our children are our joy and crown, and we thank the Lord every day for them and their children, our grandchildren. God's design for family is best, and when one is willing to follow His pattern, it works. We have made our share of mistakes, but the Lord is good, and His grace is sufficient. Because of our children's faithfulness, we now have four wonderful grandchildren, three great grandchildren, a wonderful son-in-law and daughter-in-law that we love very much. All of us have a wonderful friendship within our family. There is nothing better than having true friends.

Family and Self-Worth

The process of building self-esteem goes this way: a new reflection, a new experience, or a bit of new growth leads to a new success or failure, which in turn leads to a new or revised statement about oneself. In this fashion, each person's self-concept usually evolves throughout his lifetime. The value of a supportive family during this evolutionary process is inestimable. - Dorothy Corkille Briggs[2]

A Gallup Poll discovered what had already been suspected, that lack of self-esteem is the single most prevalent cause of:

- Alcoholism and Drug Abuse
- Criminal and anti-social behavior

- Low achievement levels in the academic world
- Break-ups in marriages and families.[3]

A child who has high self-esteem is one who can strive toward setting goals and also has the ability to reach their full potential. The child who has the desire to make their own choices and believes in the capacity to be right about their decisions is a child with high self-esteem. This is a child with hope who will continue to develop throughout their lifetime.

It is crucial that each family member understand the importance of self-esteem.

There are many ways to describe self-esteem. Dr. Edward Courtney in the ***Family Awareness Program Manual*** lists the following:

- **Self-esteem** is the degree that we feel good about ourselves. Our self-esteem simply is the product of everything we were born with plus everything we can hear, read, or believe about ourselves. Thus, low self-esteem is nothing to be ashamed of or embarrassed about, but something to be changed.
- **Self-esteem** is a concept, an attitude, a feeling, an image, represented by behavior.
- **Self-esteem** is valuing ourselves, to treat ourselves with dignity, love, and reality.
- **Our self-esteem,** at any moment, depends on what the most important person in our life feels about us.

Individuals with a strong sense of self-worth demonstrate the following qualities:

- They have a high moral and ethical sensitivity.
- They have a strong sense of family.
- They are far more successful in interpersonal relationships.
- Their perspective of success is viewed in terms of interpersonal relationships, not in materialistic terms.
- They're far more productive on the job.
- They are far lower in incidence of chemical addictions. *(In view of the fact that current research studies show that 80% of all suicides are related to alcohol and drug addiction, this becomes terribly significant.)*
- They are more likely to get involved in social and political activities in their community.
- They are far more generous to charitable institutions and give far more generously to relief causes.[4]

The characteristics of an individual who has self-esteem are integrity, honesty, responsibility, compassion, love, and competence. The individual feels that he matters. The world is a better place because of him. He feels able to make his own decisions. He radiates with trust and hope. He knows he can make a difference in this world.

When an individual feels little worth, he expects to be cheated, stepped on, and devalued by others. Expecting the worst, he invites the role of victimization. Without self-esteem he tends to distrust, becomes left out and has feelings of loneliness and isolation. It is all too common for those who suffer from lack of self-esteem to hide behind this high psychological wall and then defend themselves by denying they are really doing it to themselves.

As loving parents, we can learn to demonstrate simple techniques that will help build self-esteem in the lives of our children. One of the first steps is to value ourselves and in turn bring confidence and assurance into the lives of our children. Every word, facial expression, gesture or action as a parent gives our children some message about what we believe and think about ourselves and about them.

In the process of learning to model positive self-esteem attributes, it would be beneficial to observe the following characteristics in children with feelings of worth:

- Willing to take risks
- Outgoing
- Makes friends easily
- Makes positive statements about themselves
- Gives compliments to others easily
- Able to laugh at themselves
- Respects self, can say "no" in situations
- Understands that we learn from mistakes
- Knows we don't have to be perfect at everything

On the other hand, children in troubled families often feel worthless, growing up as they must amid "crooked" communication, inflexible rules, criticism of their differentness, punishment for their mistakes, and no experience in learning responsibility. Such children are highly at risk of developing destructive behavior toward themselves and/or others. Observable characteristics in children with feelings of worthlessness might include:

- Reluctant to take risks
- Shies away from peers
- Frequently tattles
- Brags about accomplishments
- Teases others, puts others down
- Becomes defensive
- Is easily frustrated
- Demeans own talents, continually puts self-down

These same differences in self-worth can be seen in adult family members. It is not so much that the family affects the adult's sense of self (although this certainly can happen) as this: *parents with high self-esteem are more likely to create nurturing families and low self-worth parents to produce troubled families.*[5]

There are many things we as parents, teachers and pastors can do to promote self- esteem. Creating a positive atmosphere is most important. Being tolerant of mistakes is always appropriate. Correction is necessary, but rewards are important, too. We must share our love with hugs and words of praise. Showing open love is a significant need today. This is the kind of atmosphere we need to create in our places of learning.

In troubled families:

- Self-worth is low.
- Communication is indirect, vague and not really honest.
- Rules are rigid, nonnegotiable and everlasting.
- The family's link to society is fearful, placating, and blaming.

In healthy, supportive, nurturing families:

- Self-worth is high.
- Communication is direct, clear, specific, and honest.
- Rules are flexible, appropriate, and subject to change.
- The link to society is open and hopeful and is based on choice.[6]

Of course, we all know that the perfect family does not exist. All families experience problems and changes. Every family has its own set of strengths as well as its own set of weaknesses. We do not need to focus on our weaknesses, but build on our strengths.

To change the world is to *first* change the family. Family life can be likened to an iceberg. Most of us are aware of about one-tenth of what is going on—the tenth that we can see and hear. A family's destiny depends on understanding the feelings and needs that lie beneath everyday family events.

Communication and Retention Action Steps

Preparation:

Begin by asking yourself:

Am I the kind of person who others would consider a friend?

Do I have a friend that I can think out loud with?

What have I gained through my close friendships?

Would I describe myself as having high self-esteem?

Read Proverbs 18:24.

Who is this friend?

Is He my close friend?

Do the youth in my life know He is my closest friend?

Pray and ask your Friend to help you show others the value of His unique and awesome friendship.

Communication:

There were some powerful statements made in this chapter about the importance of real friends. Ask each member of your group to share an example from one of them.

It is through our friendships that we gain some of our most needed strength.

From them we gain courage to keep moving forward.

Through special friends, we obtain needed affirmation.

Because of friends we take courage to tackle the hardest of challenges.

Because of friends we gain the wisdom to venture into the unknown.

With their help we accomplish life's impossible dreams.

What is the definition of self-esteem?

Fill in these blanks that describe a child who has high self-esteem:

He or she can strive toward setting _____ (answer: goals).

They have the ability to reach their full _____ (answer: potential).

The child has the desire to make their own _____ (answer: choices)

He or she believes in the capacity to be right about their _____ (answer: decisions). This is a child has _____ (answer: hope) for the future.

They will continue to _____ (answer: develop) throughout their lifetime.

Individuals with a strong sense of self-worth demonstrate the following qualities. Ask your group to write "Qualities of self-worth" on a piece of paper. As you read through this list, have them put a check mark every time they hear one they feel describes themselves.

- They have a high moral and ethical sensitivity.
- They have a strong sense of family.
- They are far more successful in interpersonal relationships.
- Their perspective of success is viewed in terms of interpersonal relationships, not in materialistic terms.
- They're far more productive on the job.
- They are far lower in incidence of chemical addictions.
- They are more likely to get involved in social and political activities in their community.
- They are far more generous to charitable institutions and give far more generously to relief causes.[4]

Do the same with this list of the characteristics of an individual who has self-esteem.

- Integrity
- Honesty
- Responsibility
- Compassion
- Love
- Competence
- Feels that he or she matters
- Feels the world is a better place because of him or her
- Feels able to make his or her own decisions
- Radiates with trust and hope

- Knows he or she can make a difference in this world

Do the same with this list of when an individual feels little worth:
- he expects to be cheated
- he expects to be stepped on
- he expects to be devalued by others
- Expecting the worst, he invites the role of victimization
- Without self-esteem he tends to distrust
- He becomes left out
- Has feelings of loneliness and isolation

As loving parents, we can learn to demonstrate simple techniques that will help build self-esteem in the lives of our children. One of the first steps is to value ourselves and in turn bring confidence and assurance into the lives of our children. Every word, facial expression, gesture or action as a parent gives our children some message about what we believe and think about ourselves and about them.

Retention:

There are many things we as parents, teachers, and pastors can do to promote self- esteem in our young people. Here are some to get us started.

Creating a positive atmosphere is most important.

Being tolerant of mistakes is always appropriate.

Correction is necessary but rewards are important, too.

Add to this list: _____

We must share our love with hugs and words of praise. Showing open love is a significant need today.

Discuss why this is true.

Of course, we all know that the perfect family does not exist. All families experience problems and changes. Every family has its own set of strengths as well as its own set of weaknesses. We do not need to focus on our weaknesses, but build on our strengths.

Have each parent and leader list their family's strengths.

To change the world is to *first* change the family. Family life can be likened to an iceberg. Most of us are aware of about one-tenth of what is going on—the tenth that we can see and hear. A family's destiny depends on understanding the feelings and needs that lie beneath everyday family events.

> Have your parents and leaders begin to journal the feelings and needs they see beneath the surface that they need to begin to deal with in their own families.
>
> Have them begin to compile a "to do list" as to how to deal with these issues.

Ask them to bring it to your next meeting and have a brainstorming session to help each other begin to deal with them.

Ask everyone to read the next chapter before the next meeting.

PART IV

WHAT ARE WE TO COMMUNICATE TO TODAY'S YOUTH?

Chapter 12

Principal Truths

What is Truth?

The urgent need of this very hour is to teach our youth the value of **absolute truth**. Without an understanding of what truth is, our youth cannot make sound decisions on a daily basis. Most parents do not understand the meaning of absolute truth and are not able to communicate this principle. Therefore, parents need to first learn for themselves and then teach their children that in this world where things are always changing, the truth in God's Word never changes.

One of the most superb selections I have found on the subject of absolute truth was produced by Josh McDowell and Bob Hosteller in their book, ***Right From Wrong*** (see Appendix A).

The greatest challenge of the 21st century we face as parents, teachers, and leaders of youth is teaching absolute truth. We must face the realization of the truth that King David spoke of in Psalm 11:3, "If the foundation be destroyed, what can the righteous do?" The issue biblically is the fact that the Word of God is absolute truth. The values of truth, marriage, purity, honesty, love, peace, and happiness must be built on the scriptural foundation of absolute truth.

Accepting the biblical message of truth is the starting point for teaching our youth the principles of life that will bring fulfillment and happiness in their lives. If the Bible is not accepted as the authority by which lives and futures are built, it will be difficult to relate a message that will bring effective results.

It is of utmost importance to establish a belief in the Word of God as the ultimate authority. Without the Word of God as our authority, we have no absolute truth.

All of us sense that there has been a deterioration of the truth. We are presently setting records in dishonesty, disrespect, sexual promiscuity, violence, suicide, and other pathologies. The obvious reason is we have lost our moral fiber and our belief in the foundational laws that govern the hearts of men.

The way our youth approach truth has a definite effect on their behavior, attitudes and the choices they make. We must understand that the way in which we accept an objective standard for distinguishing if something is right or wrong makes all the difference in the choices we make. If we believe there is an objective truth or standard, it makes all the difference in the world. This means that truths do not change no matter what. These are foundational truths that are derived from the Word of God which do not change for any person, any place or any time.

If our young people are going to learn right from wrong, we have the challenge of teaching them how to determine what truths are absolute and why.

Studies show that when our youth do not accept an objective standard of truth they become:

- 36% more likely to lie to you as a parent!
- 48% more likely to cheat on an exam!

- 74% more likely to watch MTV!
- 2 times more likely to try to physically hurt someone!
- 2 times more likely to watch a pornographic film!
- 2 times more likely to get drunk!
- 2 1/4 times more likely to steal!
- 3 times more likely to use illegal drugs!
- 6 times more likely to attempt suicide!

If your child fails to embrace truth as an objective standard that governs their lives, the study shows it will make them:

- 65% more likely to mistrust people!
- 2 times more likely to be disappointed!
- 2 times more likely to be angry with life!
- 2 times more likely to be lacking purpose!
- 2 times more likely to be resentful![1]

As you can see, there are no easy answers, but there *are* answers! The solutions are hard to take sometimes, but if we are willing to make a difference and do our best to communicate the truthful answers to our youth, we have the most to gain. After all, it is *our* youth whom we desire to salvage from the reeling, confused world of teenagers.

We need to teach our teens practical ways of identifying what truths are absolute.

We must give young people the information that will allow them the option of making decisions with the knowledge of right and wrong. Remembering that truth is absolute, we must go beyond treating the symptoms that are a result of this lack of knowledge. We need to teach youth the solution is far more complex than reaching for the nearest gun or taking drugs to escape the present reality. The problems of lying, pre-marital sex, cheating on exams, alcohol and drugs are never going to be under control until we teach our youth to abide by the truth. They will then have the ability to be in control of their lives.

Two Models of Truth

There is a segment of history we must be familiar with in order to properly relate to the two basic models of truth that are being examined today by our schools.

There are four different periods of history that have had a profound influence on the way our generation thinks.

The Renaissance (approximately 1300 and covering the next two centuries) began in Italy and passed through Europe, lasting through the sixteenth century. The Renaissance shifted the art, music, and literature of the Middle Ages that exalted God and His glory to that of using the arts to exalt man and his abilities. The Renaissance marked the beginning of man thinking of his own abilities rather than accepting that his ability came from God.

Following the Renaissance, the period called the Enlightenment Period, the Age of Reason made its appearance. The Enlightenment Period began in the 1600s and lasted through the next century. This was a time when men such as Voltaire and Descartes claimed that if there had been a God who created the world, He had no contact with it now. This left man to discover right and wrong for himself. During the Renaissance man (not God) became central. In the Enlightenment Period man's reasoning became predominant. It was this period's purpose to replace God's reasoning with that of man's. It was replacing reasoning which could not be understood with that which could be explained by man.

The next is the Industrial Revolution. The Industrial Revolution overlapped the Enlightenment Period, extending from the 1700s through the 1800s. This was a time of progress—invention, improvement in communication, and building factories. Along with this success came confidence in man and his abilities. Man was now looking to himself for answers. He was successful. He did not need God. Man turned inward. Charles Darwin published his theory known as *The Origin of the Species* in 1859. His theories presented an alternative to a theistic understanding of origin; God was no longer needed to explain or understand how the world and man came to be. This period of time, the Time of Darwin, completed the cycle that spawned the thinking that men and women were on their own.

They could now decide for themselves what was truth and what was morally right and wrong. Human reasoning had replaced God as the object of modern man's worship. Darwin's teachings resulted in man's becoming arrogant and self-reliant. It also resulted in God becoming unwelcome and unnecessary.

History brings us to the conclusion that we now have two models of truth. The first model of truth defines God as the One God with truth defined by Him. His truth is objective and absolute. The second model of truth is defined by individual human beings. Truth to him is subjective and situational.

The first model acknowledges that God, not man, is central, that He is the source of all things, and that He rules over all things. God is the author and judge of right and wrong.

The second model places the individual in control of moral matters. This places the standard within the individual. Each individual can decide for themselves what is right and wrong, depending on the circumstances. It is man-centered, not God-centered.

Our culture today, which was once guided by God and His precepts, has fully embraced this second model. This shift from the first model to the second has affected every aspect of society, from the arts to music to literature to politics.

Unfortunately, many of our young people are adopting the second model of thinking today. It has shaped and molded their present world and their way of thinking. It is the model that they use to make life's decisions. The Bible says of Jesus Christ, "And he is before all things and by him all things consist" (Colossians 1:17). God is the infinite source. His absolutes make sense of life. If there is no absolute moral standard, then it is impossible to distinguish right from wrong. Absolutes always apply. They provide a final or ultimate standard. In order to have morals and values, we must have absolutes. If there are no absolutes beyond our own thoughts then there is no way to make moral judgments. We only have conflicting opinions.

The Original Mode

The International Bureau of Weights and Measures has headquarters in Sevres, France. This organization standardizes units of measure, establishes standards for metric measurements, and insures a reliable standard for physical measurements around the world. To obtain the most precise measurement possible, the Bureau would be the correct place to go. To check the absolute accuracy of a millimeter ruler, comparison with standards of the Bureau would be in order.

Suppose there is a dispute over the size of our swimming pools. I say that my pool is three cubic meters larger than yours. You measure your pool with your measuring stick, and I measure mine with my measuring rod. How can we determine which pool is larger? We must compare your measuring stick and my measuring rod to the Bureau's standard, which has already been established.

Likewise, we must give our children the standard that has already been established for morals and consistency in making decisions between right and wrong. This can be accomplished by giving them a method through which they can test the truth. We need to give our youth the assurance that there is a standard that exists for determining what is morally right or wrong. They need a dependable standard; one which exists outside ourselves.

If there is a universal truth that applies to all people at all times, it must come from outside ourselves. It must come from a source other than another human being. Yet absolute truth must be common to all humanity, to all creation.

Those requirements for a standard of truth and morality are found only in one person—God. God is the source of all truth. "He is the Rock, his work is perfect... a God of truth and without iniquity, just and right is he" (Deuteronomy 32:4). God's nature and character define truth. He is the standard and defines what is right for all people, for all times, and in all places. But truth is not something He decides, it is something He is. The Apostle James wrote, "Every good gift and every perfect gift is from above, and cometh down from the Father of lights, with whom is no variableness, neither shadow of turning" (James 1:17).

The challenge is to equip our youth with knowledge based on biblical principles and reasoning. Armed with this knowledge, which is derived from truth, young people can make decisions which are in agreement with God's truth. For example, they need to understand that the reason chastity is moral and promiscuity is immoral is because God said it is. He is a pure God; therefore, we are to be pure.

The problem is that we have moved away from the original measure and chosen to measure right and wrong by the thinking and concepts of our society, which says, "If it doesn't bother someone else, then I'll just do it," or "If I think it is okay, it must be okay."

We have moved away from God and made ourselves the center of all things rather than allowing God to be the center of all things.

It is not a matter of what I think is right or what you think is wrong that matters. The question is, "What does God's Word say, and what is the nature of God in this matter?" He is just, He is love, He is pure, and He is holy.

Our children are taught that they are violating their parents' standards and codes, when in reality absolute truth is not determined by what the parent sets up as the rules. It is God and God alone who determines what is absolute truth. Truth exists because God is who He is and He is outside us, He is from above. Therefore, truth is universal; it is consistent; and it is eternal. Absolute truth is absolute because it originates from the original.

Parents must adopt God's standards in order to insure that young people understand that right and wrong are not measured by human standards, but by the nature and character of God himself. Remember, He is the originator.

Where Do We Start

Ideally, we begin teaching our children when they are preschool age about the basic principles and precepts of God. Otherwise, when they become teenagers they do not have confidence and faith in the Word of God. Then the challenge becomes much greater.

In Proverbs 1:7 Solomon states, "The fear of the Lord is the beginning of knowledge...." As many parents can attest, a child who has a true biblical understanding of the fear of God also has a faith in God, which translates into a comprehending what truth is. We need to develop a real appreciation of the power of God, what He **can** do, and what He **will** do in our lives.

When Moses approached the burning bush, he was warned by God in Exodus 3:5 "... put off thy shoes from off thy feet, for the place whereon thou standest is holy ground." Moses fell to the ground and hid his face from God. The prophet Isaiah's vision of God high and lifted up, brought Isaiah to his knees. "Woe is me... I am a man of unclean lips, a man living in the midst of an unclean people. I have seen the Lord high and lifted up" (Isaiah 6:1). The Apostle John walked with the Lord on the dusty roads of Jerusalem but when he saw Jesus after His resurrection, he fell at His feet. These men all feared the Lord, but not as though they were afraid for their lives. They had a profound awareness of God and His presence and a reverence for Him and what He could do. There are many reasons to fear the Lord God Almighty:

We must fear God because He is God. It is natural for humans to respect and admire talents and abilities beyond their own. Albert Einstein's name is famous because his intellectual brilliance seems so unattainable. Sandra Day O'Connor is admired by many as the first woman to serve on the Supreme Court. Michael Jordan became a sports icon because he performed athletic feats that seemed impossible. Yet the abilities of even the greatest among us are insignificant when compared to the might and majesty of God. He is so far removed from us in holiness, power, wisdom, and love that we cannot compare to Him; we cannot fully comprehend Him; we cannot even approach Him without mercy.

*Joshua and his generation had seen and heard
all the great works of the Lord.*

From birth their children heard stories of the mighty power of Yahweh, the God of their fathers who saved Noah and his family from the flood, who destroyed Sodom and Gomorrah for their wickedness, who gave Abraham a son in old age, who delivered Joseph out of prison, who sent plagues on the Egyptians, who parted the Red Sea, who wrote the law on tablets of stone, who brought down the walls of Jericho. They instilled within their children a reverence for the Almighty, a God of love and mercy. With every story, every ceremony, every ordinance and every Passover meal, they demonstrated their dependence on God. They acknowledged that God was infinite, and they were finite. They acknowledged that God was all-powerful, and they were weak. They acknowledged that God was all-knowing, and they lacked wisdom. They were profoundly aware of God and of their dependence upon Him.

We must fear God because He is the source of all good things. "He will fulfill the desire of them that fear him..." sang the Psalmist (Psalm 145:19). All that we are, He has made us. All that we have, He has given us. All that we lack, He can provide.

The Bible teaches that, "Every good gift and every perfect gift is from above and cometh down from the Father of lights..." (James 1:17). Imagine how it would affect our children's attitudes and behaviors if they really believed that every breath they drew, every morsel they ate, every muscle they moved, every pleasure they experienced was a gift from a powerful and loving God. Imagine the reverence and dependence on God such an attitude would produce.

We must fear God because He is the judge of good and evil. As Solomon wrote, "The conclusion, when all has been heard, is fear God and keep his commandments, because this applies to every person. Because God will bring every act to judgment, everything which is hidden, whether it is good or evil..." (Ecclesiastes 12:13-14 NASB). He will bring every act into judgment; He will measure it against Himself. If it is consistent with His own character, then it is truth, it is good; if it is not consistent with his character, then it is error, it is evil.

We must fear God because He holds the power of life and death. "The Lord preserveth all them that love him: but all the wicked will he destroy" (Psalm 145:20). Our lives are in his hands: "It is of the Lord's mercies that we are not consumed because his compassions fail not. They are new every morning: great is thy faithfulness" (Lamentations 3:22-23). When the children of Israel sang the song of Moses, they proclaimed the power of God over life and death. "See now that I, I am he, and there is no god beside me; it is I who put to death and give life..." (Deuteronomy 32:39 NASB).

We must fear God because it is for our own good. God promises blessing to those who fear and honor Him: "And they shall be my people, and I will be their God: and I will give them one heart, and one way, that they may fear me forever, for the good of them, and their children after them" (Jeremiah 32:38-39).

When my wife was a child she thought her father was the most loving yet awe- inspiring man in the world. She loved the smell of his aftershave, she loved cuddling in his strong arms, she loved playing hide and seek with him; but she also considered him the smartest, tallest, and strongest man she knew. The potent combination of love and respect delivered her from many dangers. She stayed away from the knife drawer in the kitchen. She played only where she was allowed. She ate her vegetables. You might say that her love for her father made her willing to obey him, and her fear made her unwilling to disobey him.

Similarly God wants His children to love Him wholeheartedly, but He also wants them to fear Him, to respect Him, and to reverence Him because He knows that such a potent combination of emotions will be for our own good and for the good of our children after us.

It is that fear of the Lord that we must reclaim and revive in our churches and families—and in ourselves. We must reverence Him; we must acknowledge Him. Not just in theory, but in practice. The fear of the Lord must pervade our lives; it must be in the stories we tell our children, in the way we live, in the way we think, in the way we talk. Then we will be able to better understand how to apply His truth to our lives.2

What is Morality?

The fear of the Lord is the beginning of wisdom. That is the starting point. We must move from there and give information to our children about the true nature of God and help them realize the character of God. The original truth comes from the Creator and his precepts.

From the very beginning God said to Adam and Eve that, while in the Garden of Eden, "... Of every tree of the garden thou mayest freely eat: But of the tree of the knowledge of good and evil, thou shall not eat of it: for in the day that thou eatest thereof thou shall surely die" (Genesis 2:16-17).

Adam and Eve were created by God, placed in the Garden of Eden, surrounded with all the beautiful trees and flowers, and the upkeep was their responsibility. They were given the freedom to dress it and keep it, but they were not to eat of the one tree—the tree of the knowledge of good and evil. They had a choice. They knew to do good, but to disobey meant death. They had a choice between doing right and doing wrong. By giving this first command, God identified Himself as a moral being, the defender of right and wrong. God is the source of absolute truth.

God himself placed that tree in the garden, and it became the object that decided what was right and what was wrong.

When God appeared to Adam and Eve in the garden, He called out to them; they ran and hid themselves and sewed fig leaved together to hide their nakedness. After they had disobeyed, God asked them what they had done. God was making it known that He was the lawgiver and that He was the judge of good and evil. As a righteous judge, He would be the one to bring about punishment to them by cursing them and the whole of creation and then casting them out of the garden.

When Cain slew his brother Abel, God asked him what he had done. He manifested His hate for murder, revealed Himself as the giver of life and the God of life, and cursed Cain by banishing him to the land of Nod.

Throughout the Word of God, He has revealed Himself as the source of absolute truth. Through the life of Noah, He revealed Himself as a God who rewards righteousness and punishes unrighteousness. God showed Himself to Abraham as a God who could be trusted by keeping His promises.

David was the one God used to help us understand that He is a God of mercy and forgiveness. God revealed Himself through many Bible stories to show that He is the all-powerful one who should be revered and feared. He revealed His ultimate character of love when He gave His only begotten Son Jesus Christ to be the supreme sacrifice for the sins of the world.

The origin of morality is given to us through the divine revelation of God, the Bible, Jesus' miraculous incarnation, and the life He lived while on the earth. He is the beginning of morality.

The Ten Commandments are representative of God's laws and state the most understandable laws of absolute truth in the history of the world. Remember that these laws were not an afterthought. The Ten

Commandments were given to the newborn nation of Israel to reveal God's nature and help them enjoy the benefits of moral behavior.

The Israelites were commanded to worship only God Himself because He knew the truth about all the other gods of the nation—that they were only idols. God made the heavens and the earth (Psalm 96:5).

God has told us not to kill human beings because He is the originator and creator of life (Acts 3:15). God is a God that does not lie. Because He is a God of truth, He instructs us not to lie (Titus 1:2). The commandments of God that are found in the Bible are given to us in order that we might have a practical knowledge of the character of God, that we might understand the nature of God and have the ability to live and develop a relationship with Him. His laws and commands, which we call precepts, point to His nature, and in turn, point to truth which is true for all people, for all times, in all places.

The laws He has given flow from who He is.

God is the Root of all Truth

There are two major techniques that we must communicate to our young people if we are going to give them a strong foundational footing on which to make their decisions and retain them in the future. First, we must teach the true meaning of fearing God—the reverence and respect for who He is. Second, we must communicate that He is the root, the beginning, the basis, the originator of all truth.

We have heard and possibly even said ourselves, "Because I said so!" If the youth do not respect their parents or teachers, they are going to reject their rule because they do not accept their authority. If a young person does not accept the authority of the Scripture, they will not be persuaded to avoid immorality "because the Bible says so." Our young people should be taught to reject a particular action, not because someone "said so" but because "God is like that."

In any situation, if you can determine what law or commandment applies, how it originates from God's character, and how it reflects His love and care for us, you are well on the road to developing a life that can stand in times of testing and trial.

Teaching the laws of God and His commandments is important, but we also need to teach what God is like. Teaching the character of God is teaching them the actions of God. When youth understand the Originator, they are ready to evaluate right and wrong for themselves. They must learn to evaluate on an objective basis. God has made His laws for all people, in all places and all times.

Why are drive-by killings wrong? Perhaps someone in one gang has already killed someone in another gang. Since they killed first, it must be all right. It was the general consensus of all the members.

Why is it wrong for a girl to give in to sex with her boyfriend? After all, he said he loved her, and she loves him. Everyone else is saying that it is okay. It seems like the popular thing to do.

Why is it wrong to cheat on an exam if it helps improve your grades, and no one else knows about it? It made things better for the student, the parents were happy, and a better grade was obtained.

There is a truth that is outside of us and beyond any human being. There are truths about killing, sex outside of marriage, and dishonesty that originate with God. Killing is wrong because there is a God who is the creator of life, and He has said life needs to be preserved. Premarital sex is wrong because God is a God who created sex, and He says it is only for those who are married. Cheating is wrong because God is a God of honesty, and He is a God of truth.

God is the originator of truth for the universe, the absolute standard for everything that is good and right. Without that standard, there can be no universal, absolute guidelines.

A Method That Works

Lying is wrong; stealing is wrong; hatred is wrong—not because our society or the church frown on them, but because they are contrary to the nature and character of God.

Communicating such things to a generation that is losing its moral basis can be a disheartening task. How can we communicate the Test of Truth to our children and grandchildren? It is done in much the same way as any other teaching. Your mother did not elaborate on the theory of linguistics before she taught you the alphabet. Your first grade teacher did not expound the distinction between pure mathematics and applied math before he taught you that one plus one was two. Your piano instructor mentioned nothing about chord progressions before she positioned your hands over the piano keyboard and instructed you to place your right thumb on middle C.

Communicating basic morality follows the same technique. That is why God began with the Ten Commandments. (Actually, He began with the command to Adam and Eve not to eat of the tree of the knowledge of good and evil.) God's commands, or precepts, point to universal moral principles that originate from the Person of God Himself. That is the divine pattern for teaching right and wrong, which has an objective basis in the nature and character of God.

Precept

Your first days in school may have been occupied with such mathematical concepts as one plus one equals two and two plus two equals four. Those were your baby steps in mathematics. As a five or six year old, you may have been proud of your ability to understand such quantities. Little did you know that you were not dealing in quantities, but were learning to express quantities through the use of numbers.

Similarly, few people realize that precept—the rules, regulations, codes, and requirements of Scripture—is the *first step* to understanding basic morality. God gave us specific commands to provide explicit boundaries for human conduct.

These precepts also point to greater moral principles which lead us to learn deeper lessons. The Apostle Paul wrote to the churches of Galatia, "Therefore, the law has become our tutor [literally, child-conductor] to lead us to Christ, that we may be justified by faith" (Gal. 3:24 NASB). In Paul's day, there was a type of household servant whose duty was to oversee the child's character development. He was also to take the child to school each day to ensure he was under the teacher's care.

Paul uses this example from his culture to show us that the law has the same function. The commandments and precepts of Scripture are designed not only to say, "Do this" and "Don't do that," but to lead us beyond the precept to a universal principle (one that applies to everyone) and ultimately to God.

Principle

Principles are the *intermediate steps* on the stairway that lead us from precepts to the person of God. Behind each specific command precept is a principle. A principle is a standard that can be applied to different situations. Principles help explain the why behind a command (precept). Safety is the principle behind the mother's command, "Look both ways before crossing the street." Reverence for life is the principle behind God's command, "Thou shalt not kill."

By teaching our young people the principles behind God's precepts, we equip them to apply the Test of Truth to moral matters. However, there is a greater moral truth beyond principles to which the law points, and that is the very person of God.

Person

To know God's precepts and even the principles of truth that lie behind those precepts and not know the Person from whom they are derived is worthless. Too often we focus on God's laws but never learn what it teaches about the character of God. God's ultimate purpose in every precept is to bring people to the knowledge of Himself.

Many Bible readers are tempted to skip over the Old Testament chapters which detail thousands of regulations. They seem totally irrelevant today. But these instructions reveal the character of God. The purpose of those laws was to give Israel a lesson in purity, separating good from bad, clean from unclean. The principle behind the law—purity of life—flowed from the character of God Himself. His commands were intended not only to benefit His people, but also to help them understand what He was like and that He was a God who did not tolerate sin. Their obedience to those laws was to point them to the perfect model of God's holiness.

God's law is not an end in itself. Some of His commands were illustrative, others were practical, but all were—and are—an expression of His character. King David acknowledged:

"The law of the Lord is perfect, converting the soul: the testimony of the Lord is sure, making wise the simple. The statutes of the Lord are right, rejoicing the heart: the commandment of the Lord is pure, enlightening the eyes. The fear of the Lord is clean, enduring forever: the judgments of the Lord are true and righteous altogether" (Psalm 19:7-9).

Notice the words David used to describe God's law: perfect, sure, right, pure, clean, and righteous. God Himself possesses these qualities. The truth does not reside in the commands; it resides in God, who is eternal.

We can help our youth determine right from wrong by teaching them to fear God and to look to His nature and character as the measure of truth and morality.

We help them apply the Test of Truth by asking how it compares to the original. An attitude or behavior is not wrong just because adults say it is wrong. The truth is right for all people, for all times, and in all places. Today's youth may be slow to accept this standard for determining truth. Parents and youth leaders must be prepared to offer the Test of Truth.[3]

Since many youth doubt the basics of the Word of God, other areas must be addressed as well. A good place to start with our teenagers is the area of Evidence of Truth. How do we convince doubting teenagers that they can trust the Bible and that it is a worthy standard? It is not uncommon for a teenager to ask when being witnessed to, "How can you prove the Bible to be the Word of God?" Following are some ideas on why we accept the Word of God as our standard of truth.

God is Not Doing Something to You, He is Doing Something for You

Seatbelts are a habit in my family. When our children were small, they were secured in car seats; when they were outgrew the car seat, they learned to fasten their own seatbelts. I don't recall any argument or protest from them. It was just something the family did.

When my children's younger friends rode in the car with us, however, they occasionally responded indignantly when I required them to fasten their seatbelts. I have had young people from the ages of three to twenty-three sigh loudly, roll their eyes at me, and offer heartfelt protests.

Their responses communicate that they think I'm the meanest, most demanding, most unreasonable parent they've ever met. Their attitudes reflect a belief that I'm only making them wear seat belts in order to make them miserable. That's not true, of course. I would much prefer to give in and save myself the grief their mournful cries cause, but I don't. Why? Because I know that the seatbelts could save their lives. My "safety regulations" are for their own good.

Many people—our youth included—react to God's laws the way young people react to my rules about seatbelts. They see his commands as constricting. They think that biblical morality is confining. They don't see the benefits to a moral lifestyle. They need help recognizing that God's commands, like those of a loving parent—"don't touch the stove," "look both ways before you cross the street," "eat your vegetables"—are not meant to spoil our fun and make us miserable.

God gave commands, such as "flee sexual immorality" and "Husbands, love your wives," and "You shall not commit adultery," and all other commands because he wanted to protect us and provide for us. He didn't throw those precepts into the Bible just because he liked the way they sounded; he didn't concoct those rules to be a killjoy or to throw his weight around; he gave those commands because he knew some things we didn't. He knew, for example, that sexual immorality is a path, not to pleasure and fulfillment, but to emptiness and frustration.

Moses acknowledged this truth when he challenged the nation of Israel: "And now, Israel, what does the Lord your God require from you, but to fear the Lord your God, to walk in all his ways and love him, and to serve the Lord your God with all your heart and with all your soul, and to keep the Lord's commandments and his statutes **which I am commanding you today for your good?** (Deuteronomy 10:12-13 NASB emphasis added).

God issued his *commands for our good!* Looking down from an eternal, omniscient perspective, he can see things that we cannot, and he issues precepts to protect us and provide for us. We need to reinforce over and over again to our youth that all truth coming from the absolute character of God is for their good.[4]

The Moral Maze

When my children were very young, I watched them navigate a maze at a small amusement park. The maze was sunk into a pit, so that from my vantage point above the pit, I was able to watch the children thread through it. Their confused meanderings seemed so pointless as they pursued one dead end after another. *Of course, I reflected, anyone can see the way to go from up here.*

From his vantage point, God can see the way through the moral maze so much better than we; and his commands are given to keep us from heading down dead ends. As Bill Hybel writes: The Lord tells us specifically that His commands are never burdensome (1 John 5:3). By this, He doesn't necessarily mean they're easy to keep. Rather, He's telling us that they're never foolish. They are never unnecessary or purely arbitrary. He doesn't force us to observe meaningless formalities, nor does He impose rules that have no value.

On the contrary, every guideline, every law, every imperative in the Bible was crafted in infinite wisdom. They were given not only to honor God, but to benefit us as well. The entire book of Deuteronomy, for example, is a testament to this truth. In that book Moses repeatedly states that God gave the commandments for our good and promises to bless us if we obey them.

"For I know the plans I have for you," God says in his word, "plans to prosper you and not to harm you, plans to give you hope and a future" (Jeremiah 29:11 NIV). His desire is that people "will always fear me for their own good and for the good of their children after them... I will rejoice in doing them good" (Jeremiah 32:39, 41a NIV). Choosing right instead of wrong does not sap all the fun and excitement out of life; on the contrary, it accomplishes our good, because God's definition of absolute truth is based on his perspective, on his knowledge of what will protect us and provide for us.

While the majority of our youth (57%) acknowledge that "God established the limits for humankind," and that "acting in conflict with his laws has negative consequences for those people," they do not appear to apply that belief to their own behavior. The Evidence of Truth helps youth to do that, it explores the consequences of an action, and whether those consequences "give you hope and a future," or whether they bring frustration and disappointment. It looks at real things—at actions and consequences—and evaluates behavior in light of the short-term and long-term results.[5]

A Word of Warning

You may at times ask the question, "Why is this happening to me?" There may be circumstances in your life that you don't understand. You may have tried to do the right thing and may have given the Lord first place (to the best of your ability), yet trials have come. Remember that just because the right decision was made does not ensure that everything will turn out the way you planned. Bad things do happen to good people and, in turn, good things happen to bad people. The Prophet Jeremiah asked, "... Wherefore doth the way of the wicked prosper?" (Jeremiah 12:1). King David confessed, "I have seen the wicked in great power, and spreading himself like a green bay tree" (Psalm 37:35). It is not a given fact that morality is always rewarded and immorality is always punished—at least here on this earth. The Bible does tell us that there is pleasure in sin for a season and that the consequences of wrong will be reckoned with, but it may not be in this lifetime. Josh McDowell writes, "The point of offering evidence for truth to young people is not that the benefits or consequences of a belief or behavior make that thing right or wrong, but it can help them learn to distinguish right from wrong... and, of course, choose that which is right. This is ultimately, the purpose of evaluating actions according to the test, "How does it correspond to reality?"[6]

The Challenge of Cyberspace to Truth and Reality

We are beginning to recognize that the Internet and communication through the worldwide web has not only increased but also, in many places and relationships, reduced or even replaced personal, face-to-face communication between people. E-mail, Facebook, Twitter, blogs, chat rooms, communicating with people behind avatars in gaming, Internet dating, Facetiming, Skype, and a multitude of other means of cyberspace communication have greatly impacted not only how we communicate but the way we communicate.

Space doesn't permit me to detail all the possibilities and dangers associated with cyberspace communication, but allow me before concluding this book, to make some observations.

1. *The Internet is real but not reality; it contains facts and truth but isn't Truth.* Commercials and conventional wisdom often perpetuate the myth or virtual reality that everything you read on the Internet must be truth because it's on the Internet. Of course, we know that evil people, pedophiles, con artists, and all sorts of evil people lurk behind false identities and alluring websites. On the other hand, much valuable and truthful information and ministry in Christ's name is also done via the web. To our alarm at times, we hear of teens bullying one another on Facebook even to the point of some teens being pushed into suicide. Parents, schools, and the Church must screen, filter, and educate youth in using the tools and apps provided on their devices in healthy, positive, truthful, wise, and Christ-like ways.

2. *Posts, Texts, Instant Messages, Blogs, Websites and all forms of cyber-communication authored by believers must speak life and not death; truth not myth; be edifying not defaming; and encouraging in love not discouraging in acrimony.* Speaking the truth in love applies to all forms of interpersonal communication whether through devices or face to face. At times, the cryptic messages written in emails or texts fail to convey the true feelings and motives behind the message. Adults must both set the example of the right way to communicate in person or through cyberspace for youth and intentionally teach children and youth how to communicate appropriately in all ways.

3. *We must guard the eye and ear gates as well as the heart.* Parents, schools, and the Church have an obligation to screen and filter all forms of communication coming through the web, the media, and cultural authority figures. We must verify the integrity of the communicators to our youth as well as the sources developing the communication. Parents cannot allow electronic devices like smart phones, tablets, computers, televisions, radios, and gaming platforms to babysit or constantly entertain children. So let's ask the question, "Do we want Disney, Pixar, Liongate, PBS, Netflix, Amazon, Apple, Google, Facebook, Twitter, an app, a gaming platform, graphic novels, or any communication source bombarding our children and teens with millions of words, gigabites, or visual images and imparting values, while Christian adults—parents, teachers, and Church leaders are rarely getting a word or the Word deposited in the hearts of children and teens?" The input of all these cyberspace sources should be controlled and guarded by the Christian adults. Failure to screen the sources and guard our children's hearts opens them up to lies, half-truths or myths, and destructive, addictive, and discouraging attacks from the world and the enemy of our souls. So if the number of hours that cyberspace is communicating to our children far exceeds our personal, godly, and loving communication, who will ultimately win their hearts, minds, and souls?

4. *Maximize the communication potential of devices.* The good news is that parents, educators, and church leaders can talk often, stay in touch with, and use all the communication tools offered on apps, the web, and through phones to communicate virtually anytime and about anything with youth. Send affirming texts. Choose positive and educational apps for your children to learn from

and search out good information about God's creation and His Word. "Facetime" on your phone or computer with youth, children, grandchildren, students, etc. The potential is that you can communicate more not less with youth and children if you make a plan and are intentional. Remember all the principles of good communication I have shared throughout this book.

I want us to remember Deuteronomy 6:4-9:

"Hear, O Israel: The LORD our God, the LORD is one. Love the LORD your God with all your heart and with all your soul and with all your strength. These commandments that I give you today are to be upon your hearts. Impress them on your children. Talk about them when you sit at home and when you walk along the road, when you lie down and when you get up. Tie them as symbols on your hands and bind them on your foreheads. Write them on the doorframes of your houses and on your gates."

This text speaks emphatically for us about continual, ongoing, face-to-face communication. God's ways are imparted to children through their parents in personal, dynamic, and sensory ways. While our electronic devices can supplement same time, and same space communication, they can never replace it or take a second place to it.

Truthfully, I could write chapters and books focused on the issues and practical communication principles and tools needed just to address the challenges raised by cyberspace communication. Before concluding this book on communication, I felt it was important to raise some of the big issues and questions. I challenge the next generation of Christian leaders, parents, and teachers to address the challenges and to overcome the enemies of the faith on this new battleground of communication—cyberspace!

Communication and Retention Action Steps

Preparation:

Begin by asking yourself:

> *Do I really believe God gave us His commands for my own good?*
>
> *Do I truly accept the Word of God as my standard of truth?*
>
> *Do I believe God made His laws for all people, in all places, and all times?*
>
> *Does reverential fear of God pervade my life?*
>
> *Is it in the stories I tell, in the way I live, think, and talk?*
>
> *Do I have a real appreciation of the power of God, what He **can** do, and what He **will** do in my life?*

Read Deuteronomy 32:4.

God's nature and character define truth. He is the standard and defines what is right for all people, for all times, and in all places.

Pray

Communication:

We need to reinforce over and over again to our youth that all truth coming from the absolute character of God is for their good.

Can we honestly tell them that an attitude or behavior is not wrong just because adults say it is wrong?

Can we prove to them that real truth is right for all people, for all times, and in all places?

To know God's precepts and even the principles of truth that lie behind those precepts and not know the Person from whom they are derived is worthless.

Why?

Too often we focus on God's laws but never learn what it teaches about the character of God. God's ultimate purpose in every precept is to what?

By teaching our young people the principles behind God's precepts, we equip them to apply the Test of Truth to moral matters.

Behind each specific command precept is a _____.

What is a principle? (Answer: It is a standard that can be applied to different situations. Principles help explain the why behind a command or precept).

Can you explain why God gave us specific commands?

(Answer: to provide explicit boundaries for human conduct.)

Some examples are:

> Killing is wrong because _____ (answer: there is a God who is the creator of life, and He has said life needs to be preserved.)
> Premarital sex is wrong because _____ (answer: God is a God who created sex, and He says it is only for those who are married.)
> Cheating is wrong because _____ (answer: God is a God of honesty, and He is a God of truth.)

God is the originator of truth for the universe, the absolute standard for everything that is good and right. Without that standard, there can be no universal, absolute guidelines.

Teaching the laws of God and His commandments is important, but we also need to teach what God is like. Teaching the character of God is teaching them the actions of God.

> Why? (answer: When youth understand the Originator, they are ready to evaluate right and wrong for themselves.)

There are two major techniques that we must communicate to our young people if we are going to give them a strong foundational footing on which to make their decision and retain them in the future.

First, we must teach the true meaning of fearing God—the reverence and respect for who He is.

> Discuss ways to do this.

Second, we must communicate that He is the root, the beginning, the basis, the originator of all truth.

> Discuss ways to do this.

The Bible teaches that, "Every good gift and every perfect gift is from above and cometh down from the Father of lights..." (James 1:17).

How would it affect our children's attitudes and behaviors if they really believed that every breath they drew, every morsel they ate, every muscle they moved, every pleasure they experienced was a gift from a powerful and loving God?

What would such an attitude produce?

Retention:

Parents must adopt God's standards in order to insure that young people understand that right and wrong are not measured by human standards, but by the nature and character of God himself. They must be taught by not only our words but our actions that we believe He is the originator.

We must teach them that it is not a matter of what I think is right or what you think is wrong that matters. The question is, "What does God's Word say, and what is the nature of God in this matter?"

To do this we must become knowledgeable about God's Word and be willing to take the time to look an issue up in His Word when it comes under discussion with our youth. We cannot respond with, " Because I told you so." We must be able to prove that it is from God's Word.

The challenge is to equip our youth with knowledge based on biblical principles and reasoning. Armed with this knowledge, which is derived from truth, young people can then make decisions which are in agreement with God's truth.

Those requirements for a standard of truth and morality are found only in one person—God. God is the source of all truth and our reference book is the Bible.

Our youth must be taught how to seek the answers from God's Word.

Teach them how to use a concordance and a Bible Dictionary or to look things up on line at a reliable source.

We need to give our youth the assurance that there is a standard that exists for determining what is morally right or wrong. They need a dependable standard; one which exists outside ourselves.

We must become the guardians of all that enters the minds and hearts of our children and youth including the new sources of information coming from cyberspace. We must supervise and screen information for truth and integrity instead of letting cyberspace control the flow of information to our children.

God is the infinite source. His absolutes make sense of life. If there is no absolute moral standard, then it is impossible to distinguish right from wrong. Absolutes always apply and provide a final or ultimate standard. In order to have morals and values, we must have absolutes. If there are no absolutes beyond our own thoughts then there is no way to make moral judgments. We only have conflicting opinions.

God, not man, is to be the source of all things, and He rules over all things. God is the author and judge of right and wrong.

Conclusion

*O*ur challenge throughout this study has been to show that there is a major crisis in the retention of our youth in the mainstream of Christian ethics and principles. We are losing youth from our churches because we have not given them the proper example and the teaching necessary to build their lives on a solid foundation. "If the foundations be destroyed, what can the righteous do?" (Psalm 11:3).

Note that two out of five (38%) say that lying is sometimes necessary. Nearly half say they would base their choices in moral matters on feelings and emotions. For instance, one in three (33%) say they would make choices, in any given situation, based on their feelings at that moment. One in five (22%) say they would act according to "whatever feels... right," as long as no one got hurt in the process. One in seven (18%) would not turn to the Bible for guidance in moral decisions; they say the Bible does not provide people with practical standards for living. Taken altogether, about half of our youth display confusion when answering questions pertaining to ethics and morality.[1]

There are four major areas of concern when addressing the issue of communication with today's youth and their retention for tomorrow's church.

1. **We must be aware of the facts.** Our youth need us to realize from where they are coming. Most adults have not taken the time to obtain this information.

Most teens perceive themselves to be curious (89%), busy (81%), and religious (60%). They are about evenly divided as to whether they are conservative (52% say they are) or liberal (48%). Less than half say they are traditional (42%). Considerably fewer teens describe themselves as born-again Christians (33%), stressed out (25%), or lonely (13%).[2]

It is the opinion of this writer that until the adults become aware of the facts, it will be impossible to communicate the lessons and values that are necessary to produce stability and consistency. Not only must adults be equipped with the reality of the teenage world, but they must also develop the necessary skills that will allow them to communicate the message to our youth.

Young people, most of whom are not even in the work force yet, generally feel confused about life. Perplexingly, while about half claimed they were content, half also admitted to being stressed out! Large proportions described themselves as being too busy, consistently tired, temperamental, and even lazy. At least one out of every four teens stated that they were angry with life, lonely, skeptical, and mistrusting. One out of every five said they were unmotivated, resentful, and lacking in purpose.[3]

2. **Another important element of this project was to suggest methods and techniques that would answer the question, "How Do We Communicate With Today's Youth?"** Three major thoughts were given in regard to communication with today's youth, if our message is to be received.

To begin communication, we must show our interest and enthusiasm for their lives and their problems. Excitement about their lives is essential. Our conversation must have inspiration at the outset.

After developing an element of inspiration, it becomes our challenge to communicate with enthusiasm. It does not matter whether it is within a small group, a large group, or one-on-one. We must impart our information in the atmosphere of inspiration and enthusiasm.

After we have created an atmosphere of acceptance and challenge and have presented the information, our next goal is to give instruction. Here we have the opportunity to show our youth how information applies to life. There is an element in this third stage of communication that is critical, and that is the technique of "follow me."

3. **This section of material involved the subject "Where Do We Communicate with Today's Youth?"** There are four primary areas of contact with our young people in today's society.

The first area was within the family. Parents have the major responsibility of recapturing the lives of their teenagers. It is not too late. According to George Barna's in *The 1994 Churched Youth Survey,* (90%) of our churched youth affirm that they believe God's intention was for marriage to last a lifetime.[4] The significant concept in this section is that we learn within the framework of the family to take time to be together and to communicate.

The second place we find communication is within the church. The church must take time to create and teach programs that communicate truth and moral values. Our youth need to be equipped with solid, foundational views about truth and morality. All our labor is in vain if we do not invest the time it takes to introduce our youth to the person of all truth, Jesus Christ. Churches communicate the absolute truth, and it is through this teaching that values are developed which bring about maturity and long lasting results.

The third area of communication is within the school. Peers play a major role in influencing the lives of young people. Unfortunately, many young people submit to the demands of their peers. For the most part, schools have not been a positive influence in the lives of our youth.

4. **Finally, this project considers, "What Do We Communicate?"**
    What is absolute truth and why it is important in the future development of our youth? Without the ability to determine right from wrong, our youth have no future. It is crucial that our youth develop a foundation that is solidly built on values and principles.

Our challenge is to know God—to fear God for who He is and fear Him because of His characteristics and attributes. It is through Him that we determine what is right and what is wrong. When adults learn to model Him and His precepts and the truth of His Word and then communicate these truths, then and only then are we going to retain our youth for tomorrow's church.

Appendix A

Right from Wrong

$\mathscr{A}$ friend of mine once contemplated buying the home next to his as an investment property. He lived in an area of town that had seen better days; the house next door had been occasionally rented to drug dealers and users, and had regularly been the site of domestic squabbles that required police intervention. Several times gunfire had sounded in the house or the yard.

My friend hoped that buying the house, investing "sweat equity" into it, and then renting it to good tenants would allow him to improve his neighborhood - and protect his family.

He persuaded one of his in-laws, who had experience in construction and home improvement, to walk through the house with him and help spot any potential problems. The building was in deplorable condition, and while my friend was disappointed at the amount of work the house required, he remained hopeful—until they entered the basement. There, his companion pointed out gaping cracks in the foundation and sagging support structure. "This place is falling down," his companion told him. "Nothing you fix up there"—he pointed his index finger to the upper floors—"will be worth a dime because of what's wrong down here."

He pronounced his judgment that the house would probably have to be condemned—because the foundation was cracked and crumbling.

That house provides an apt illustration of the problems that face your family and mine. We all sense that something is happening to the moral foundations of our culture. Has teen pregnancy increased over 500 percent in the past 40-50 years due to a lack of sex education? Has suicide among young people increased 300 percent in less than thirty years because we live in a more complex, stressful society? Is violence, drive-by shootings, and guns in schools a result of ineffective gun-control laws? Or is there something more fundamental, more foundational at work here? I believe such problems stem from a much deeper root cause. I believe it goes deep into the very foundation of what people in our society—and in our homes—believe, and how they look at the world.

Our craving for instant gratification and easy solutions will not help us here. We won't find an answer for adolescent violence at drive-through windows; a stop at a convenience store won't keep our children from lying and cheating; we cannot solve our teen sexuality crisis in the space of a sixty-minute television program. We must dig deep. We must look beyond the symptoms and deal with the fundamental root causes.

I believe that one of the prime reasons this generation is setting new records for dishonesty, disrespect, sexual promiscuity, violence, suicide, and other pathologies, is because they have lost their moral underpinnings, their foundational belief in morality and truth has been eroded. As journalist Rowland Nethaway said, they "don't seem to know right from wrong."

Once upon a time, children were raised in an atmosphere that communicated absolute standards for behavior: certain things were right and certain things were wrong. A child's parents, teachers, ministers, youth workers, and other adults collaborated in an effort to communicate that the former should be heeded and the latter should be avoided. At one time, our society, by and large, explained the universe, humanity, and the purpose of life from the Judeo-Christian tradition: a belief that truth existed, and everyone could know and understand it. A clear understanding of what was right and wrong gave society a moral standard by which to measure crime and punishment, business ethics, community values, character and social conduct. It became the lens through which society viewed law, science, art, politics—the whole of culture. It provided a cohesive model that promoted the healthy development of the family, united communities, and encouraged responsibility and moral behavior.

That has changed drastically, however. Our children are being raised in a society that has largely rejected the notions of truth and morality, a society that somewhere lost the ability to decide what is true and what is right. Truth has become a matter of taste; morality has been replaced by individual preference.

Today's youth are being raised in a culture that reflects Hugh Hefner's "Playboy Philosophy," the creed that "if it feels good, do it." Our children seldom hear the words "right" and "wrong" from Hollywood, Nashville, and Madison Avenue; instead, they are bombarded with thousands of hours of sounds and images that glamorize immorality and mock biblical values.

Our youth are being educated in schools that profess to offer "Value free-morally neutral" rights. "We cannot tell you," the teachers and textbooks say, "what is wrong and what is right. You must decide for yourself. We can only make you aware of all the options." William J. Bennett (former secretary of education), in his book, *The De-Valuing of America*, quotes a 1985 New York Times article.

The article told of one counseling session involving fifteen high school juniors and seniors. In the course of that session a student concluded that a fellow student had been foolish to return one thousand dollars she found in a purse at school. According to the article, when the youngsters asked the counselor's opinion, "He would not try to force his values on them.' If I come from the position of what is right and what is wrong,' he explained, 'then I'm not their counselor.'"

It's not hard to see that such messages are not value-neutral at all; they teach relativism - the belief that what is true for you may not be true for me. If a counselor tells a teen that what is right or wrong is completely their decision, that counselor is conveying a philosophy that denies the existence of ultimate standards of truth and morality.

Count on it—if they have not already done so, your children will soon encounter an educational environment that rejects the notion of truth. The opening sentence of Allan Bloom's book, ***The Closing of the American Mind***, states, "There is one thing a professor can be absolutely certain of: almost every student entering the university believes, or says he believes, that truth is relative." A great many high schools and universities today not only reinforce and advance such thinking; they have evolved from institutions that aid in a search for knowledge to institutions that deny the possibility of knowing anything objectively! In such a climate, it is not surprising that seventy percent (70%) of today's generation (both churched and non-churched youth) claim that absolute truth does not exist, that all truth is relative. Most of them say that everything in life is negotiable, and that "nothing can be known for certain except the things that you experience in your own life." In other words, they don't believe that anything can be definitely defined as right or wrong. This view has been expressed to me over and over, by parents and young people alike, who refer to a certain behavior, and say, "I feel it's wrong—for me— but people have to decide for themselves whether it's wrong for them; I can't push my beliefs on others." There is much to be said for respecting others' views, of course. But our society has so emphasized personal choice and tolerance that practically an entire generation of young people have rejected an absolute standard for right and wrong. And this thinking has greatly affected your children and mine.

What emerges from the data is a portrait—of our own churched youth—of ambivalence and confusion regarding truth. An intense emotional and intellectual (and, perhaps, spiritual) battle is raging within them. A significant portion of our youth - better than half - acknowledge the existence of truth in certain circumstances, but then deny that view when the question is phrased differently. For example, seventy-two percent (72%) say that the Bible provides a clear and indisputable description of moral truth; yet only forty-four percent (44%) assert that humans are capable of grasping the meaning of truth. Apparently, they recognize there is a relationship between God's Word and moral truth, but their answers to other questions reveal a high level of confusion about that relationship.

Our survey included seven statements about objective standards of truth and morality. The reactions to the statements reveal that our young people are not at all sold on the Biblical view of right and wrong. For example, fifty-seven percent (57%) of our young people cannot even say that an objective standard of truth exists. Though that percentage is not as high as among unchurched youth, it reveals that even if your children are actively involved in church, they are likely to approve the view that "there is no such thing as absolute truth; people may define truth in contradictory ways and still be correct."

Only fifteen percent (15%) of churched youth disagree with the statement: "What is right for one person in a given situation might not be right for another person who encounters the same situation." In other words, eighty-five percent (85%) of churched youth are liable to reason, "Just because it's wrong for you doesn't mean it's wrong for me." Their idea of the distinction between right and wrong is fluid, something that is subject to change, something that is relative and personal—not constant and universal.

A mere twenty-nine percent (29%) disagreed with the statement: "When it comes to matters of morals and ethics, truth means different things to different people; no one can be absolutely positive they have the truth." This means that less than one in three of our youth believe that recognizable standards of right and wrong apply to everyone.

Just over one-third (38%) of our youth disagreed with the statement: "Nothing can be known for certain except the things that you experience in your life." Such matters as morality and ethics are up in the air for two-thirds of churched youth.

Forty-five percent (45%) of our churched youth could not disagree with the statement, "Everything in life is negotiable." The astounding implication of that statistic is that almost half of our young people are unable or unwilling to recognize some things in life as non-negotiable. It's unlikely, of course, that they realize the devastating effects of such a view, but that's part of the whole problem.

More worrisome than any single response, however, is the fact that, on a cumulative basis, only nine percent (9%) of our churched youth provided a "pro-truth" reply to each of the seven statements. In other words, less than one in ten could articulate a cohesive, consistent view of objective morality!

As we examine our children's views about truth and morality, it is apparent that the foundations upon which many parents, pastors, and youth leaders attempt to build are crumbling. Traditional Biblical concepts are eroding; a Judeo-Christian world view is being undermined. Most of our youth lack the most basic moral perspectives that previous generations took for granted. Many of our young people are struggling with the concept of truth and how they are to apply it to their own life and experience. Their inconsistent response to the above statements reveals that, even when they express a "pro-truth" position, they do so with little conviction or assurance. Our youth are confused about what truth is and who defines it; they are uncertain about what truths are absolute and what makes them absolute. Consequently, they are making conditional decisions, choosing what seems to be the best alternative at the time, without reference to any fundamental set of precepts or underlying principles to guide their behavior.

Many of our youth simply do not understand or accept absolute truth - that is, that which is true for all people, for all times, in all places. Absolute truth is truth that is objective, universal, and constant.

We all have established various family rules and guidelines. For example, I have established a curfew with my thirteen-year-old daughter, specifying what time she should be home after a football game. I have told her, "It is not good to stay out beyond eleven p.m." I have set a firm guideline to be followed. If she obeys the curfew, she is right; if she violates it, she is wrong. I want my daughter to consider it a hard and fast rule. And, in most cases she does.

But should we consider the guideline—to be home by eleven p.m. after every football game - an absolute truth? No. It is not applicable to all people, at all times, in all places. Communities, states, and governments may create various ordinances, regulations, and laws that are to be obeyed, but they are not necessarily absolutes.

Ordinances change, regulations expire, and some laws only apply in certain states. In fact, even the curfew law for my daughter may change someday. An absolute truth, on the other hand, is objective, universal, and constant.

If our children are going to learn how to determine right from wrong, they must know what truths are absolute and why. They need to know what standards of behavior are right for all people, for all times, in all places. They need to know who determines truth—and why.

The study indicates that when our youth do not accept an objective standard of truth they become:

- 36% more likely to lie to you as a parent!
- 48% more likely to cheat on an exam!
- 74% more likely to watch MTV!
- 2 times more likely to try to physically hurt someone!
- 2 times more likely to watch a pornographic film!
- 2 times more likely to get drunk!
- 2 1/4 times more likely to steal!
- 3 times more likely to use illegal drugs!
- 6 times more likely to attempt suicide!

If your child fails to embrace truth as an objective standard that governs their lives, the study shows it will make them:

- 65% more likely to mistrust people!
- 2 times more likely to be disappointed!
- 2 times more likely to be angry with life!
- 2 times more likely to be lacking purpose!
- 2 times more likely to be resentful!

How our youth think about truth has a definite effect on their behavior, the choices they make, and the attitudes they adopt.

But what is it about truth that affects behavior? It works like this. When you believe there exists an objective standard for distinguishing right from wrong—that certain things are right for all people, for all times, in all places—you acknowledge that there are fundamental moral and ethical guidelines that exist independently of your personal opinion. You acknowledge that the distinction between right and wrong is objective (it is defined outside ourselves—it is not subjectively determined), universal (it is for all people in all places—it does not change from person to person or place to place), and constant (it is for all times—it does not change from day to day). When you accept an objective standard for truth, you adopt a moral and ethical viewpoint that guides your choices of what is right and what is wrong. Youth "truth view" acts as a lens through which you see all of life and its many choices.

In the sixties and seventies, various cereal manufacturers attracted young customers with a "Hidden Picture" on the back of the cereal box. The hidden picture depicted an intricately drawn scene; but the instructions on the back of the box revealed that another picture lay hidden within that scene. The only way to discern the "Hidden Picture" was with a pair of colored spectacles that were buried inside the box (usually at the bottom). Once a young girl or boy dug those magic lenses out and slipped them on, the picture miraculously appeared in place of the old one. So it is, when a person views life through the lens of truth, they are better able to discern the "hidden" truth and distinguish what is right from what is wrong. When our youth are equipped with the proper "truth view," they will be better able to identify what truths are absolute and what makes them absolute... and they will have a fighting chance to make the right choices.

The reason, then, that youth who do not accept objective truth are more likely to lie, cheat, or get drunk, is because they are seeing their choices through faulty lenses; they have embraced a world view about truth that blinds them to the difference between right and wrong, the difference between the counterfeits and the real thing.

Many of our churched youth today believe lying to a parent can be justified, or cheating can help them get ahead, or stealing can help even the score. But you say, "Can't they see how wrong they are or how much pain they cause?" No, most of them can't, because from their point of view everything is negotiable. If the circumstances warrant it, they think their actions are justified. They are thinking and living from a difference perspective, a perspective that keeps right and wrong fluid and changing. But this way of thinking actually fools them into believing wrong choices are "right" ones. Consequently, they are accepting the counterfeits and think they are getting the real thing.

Most of the counterfeits our young people are accepting offer immediate "benefits," while right choices seem to offer more long-range benefits. Sin is packaged very appealingly in our culture, and it carries a promise of immediate satisfaction. That is why so many choose sin—it offers instant gratification. Right choices, on the other hand, often require postponing immediate satisfaction for better long-term benefits. Truth has a tough time competing with counterfeits for this reason. But a counterfeit is still a counterfeit—a substitute for the original. And far too many of our youth are suffering the consequences of choosing harmful substitutes.

I received a letter from a Christian father who had heard me speak. He said that he and his wife had always done their best to be good parents. They were members of a good church, and had always been proud of their children. But he told me that they had just discovered something about their oldest daughter, something that brought their world crashing down around them. He described his daughter as a pretty girl, but said that she'd never been real popular with boys, until recently.

She started dating one of the boys on the football team, and—this father had just learned—very early in the relationship she had sex with him. She went from that football player to another. Before long, she had slept with the whole football team! This tortured parent wrote me, "Josh, they were passing my little girl around as some sort of 'team girl!'" When these parents learned of their daughter's behavior, it had been going on for months. They sat down with their daughter and told her they knew what had been going and cried with her. Then they asked her why - "Why did you do this?" The only explanation she offered was, "I just wanted to feel loved. It never lasted for very long, and I always felt bad about it afterward, but at least for a few fleeting moments I felt like someone loved me."

My heart goes out to that girl and her parents. I can't tell you how many times I've heard similar stories—firsthand, that would melt even the hardest heart.

Sometime ago a teenage girl named Monica wrote me a poetic, but heart-wrenching letter. She penned, "Sex gave me the loneliest thrills I had ever experienced. It handed me fear as a gift and shame to wear as a garment. It blinded my eyes with false love and gave me a jagged tear in my heart...."

That letter might have been written by your daughter—or mine. Our youth don't want "a few fleeting moments" or the lonely thrills they get from a "false love"—they want the real thing. Without solid convictions about truth, however, our children will buy the counterfeits almost every time. It's like a downward spiral. When they reject truth as an objective standard, their view of life becomes distorted. When their view becomes distorted, they accept the counterfeits. When they accept the counterfeits, they begin to make wrong choices. When they make wrong choices, they suffer the consequences. The choice is, quite literally, truth or consequences.

If s a frightening prospect to raise our children in the midst of a "perverse and crooked generation." King David's words are as relevant today as they were when he first asked, "If the foundations be destroyed, what can the righteous do?" (Psalm 11:3). There are no easy answers, but there is hope. It is not too late to reinforce the crumbling foundations. If you and I are willing to set aside the "quick fix" mentality and face the stark reality of what we as a Christian community have allowed (and perhaps unwittingly adopted ourselves), I believe there is hope. But it won't be easy.

I have no miracle cure for our corrupt culture. I cannot offer sure-fire methods with a "money back guarantee" for raising children. We live in an imperfect world and none of us are perfect parents, pastors, teachers, or youth workers. Even youth from the best of families and the best of churches make tragic mistakes. Ultimately, each of your children will make their own decision regarding truth.[1]

Appendix B

Resources for Ministering to and Communicating with Youth

This resource list provided by: Luther Seminary
> http://www.luthersem.edu/cyf/children/web_sites.aspx#family

Youth and Family Ministry
> Princeton Theological Seminary Institute for Youth Ministry
> http://www.ptsem.edu/iym/

> Family Based Youth Ministry
> http://www.familybasedym.com/

> Youth and Family Institute
> http://www.youthandfamilyinstitute.org

> Huntington College Link Institute for youth ministry
> http://www.linkinstitute.com/

> Peer Ministry
> http://www.peerministry.org/

> Youthworker Journal articles
> http://www.youthspecialties.com/articles/index.php

Youth Ministry Resources

http://www.youthpastor.com/

Urban Youth Workers Institute

http://www.uywi.org/

Center for Parent/Youth Understanding

http://www.cpyu.org/

Network on Transitions to Adulthood

http://www.transad.pop.upenn.edu/index.htm

Family Ministry: Empowering Through Faith articles

http://www.familyandcommunityministries.org/

Center for Youth and Family Ministry

http://www.cyfm.net/

Center for Family & Community Ministries Baylor University

http://www.baylor.edu/cfcm

The Source for Youth Ministry ideas

http://www.thesource4ym.com/

Youth Ministry Resources

http://www.youthpastor.com/

Resource List of 6000 websites of interest to youth pastors

http://www.youthpastor.com/Resource/

Faith Inkubators

http://www.faithink.com/

Way to Live: Christian Practices for Teens

http://www.waytolive.org/

MethodX: The Way of Christ

http://www.methodx.org/

On-Line Devotions Upper Room Ministries Devo'zine

http://devozine.upperroom.org/

Practicing Our Faith

http://www.practicingourfaith.org/

TalkPoints (relationship building)

www.talkpoints.com

Youth Leadership

youthleadership.org

Research: Children, Youth, and Family Ministry

National Study of Youth and Religion Resources and additional surveys and Youth Ministry Websites

http://youthandreligion.nd.edu/related-resources/

http://www.youthandreligion.org/resources/surveys.html

Faith Factors Research

http://www.faithfactors.com/index.htm

Search Institute
http://www.search-institute.org/

Study of Exemplary Congregations in Youth Ministry
http://www.exemplarym.org/

Youth and Religion Research Project
http://www.uic.edu/depts/soci/yrp/comp/pages/home.html

Barna Research
https://www.barna.org/

Research on Religion and Families from Hartford
http://hirr.hartsem.edu/research/research_religion_family_
research.html

Brain Connection Library
http://www.brainconnection.com/library/

Fuller Youth Institute
http://fulleryouthinstitute.org

Denominational Websites about Children and Youth

National Federation for Catholic Youth Ministry
http://www.nfcym.org/

Roman Catholic
http://www.usccb.org/cchd/youth.shtml

Episcopal Church
http://www.episcopalchurch.org/page/youth-ministries

Evangelical Lutheran Church in America
http://www.elca.org/en/Our-Work/Congregations-and-Synods/
Youth-Ministry http://www.elcaymnet.org/

ELCA synod Resource Center
http://synodresourcecenter.org/

ELCA Outdoor Ministries
http://www.elca.org/camps/

Missouri Synod Lutheran Church
http://www.lcms.org/page.aspx?pid=190

Assembly of God National Youth Ministries
http://www.ag.org/youth/

United Methodist Church
http://www.gbod.org/minister-to-people/childrens-ministry
http://www.gbod.org/lead-your-church/christian-education
http://archives.umc.org/frames.asp?url=http%3A//www.
umyouth.org/

Wesleyan Church
http://wesleyankids.org/
United Church of Christ
http://www.ucc.org/youth/index.html

Presbyterian Church
http://www.pcusa.org/youthministry/

Greek Orthodox
http://www.goarch.org/en/archdiocese/departments/
greekeducation/
http://www.goarch.org/en/archdiocese/departments/youth/

Southern Baptist Convention
http://www.sbc.net/

Unitarian Universalist
http://www.uua.org/re/
http://www.uua.org/re/families/index.shtml

Coalition for the Advancement of Jewish Education
http://www.caje.org/

Children With Special Needs

Elizabeth M. Boggs Center on Developmental Disabilities
http://rwjms.rutgers.edu/boggscenter/

Faith Ability: Religion, Spirituality, and Disability
http://www.faithability.org/

United Methodist Church Disabilities Concerns
http://www.umdisabilityministries.org/ministry/umw.html

The Center for the Study of Religion and Disability
http://www.jeffmcnair.com/CSRD/

Reformed Church in America Disability Resources
https://www.rca.org/disability

Worship and Children

Bibliography of Resources for Intergenerational Worship from Calvin Institute of Christian Worship.
http://webapps.calvin.edu/worship/worshipers/intergen/intergen_bib.php

Wonderful collection of worship resources
http://webapps.calvin.edu/worship/
http://webapps.calvin.edu/worship/resources/
http://webapps.calvin.edu/worship/worshipers/children/resources.php

The Text This Week Revised Common Lectionary
http://www.textweek.com/

Environmental Issues

Earth Ministry Annotated Bibliography & Congregation Resources
http://earthministry.org/resources

Earth Charter Initiative
http://www.earthcharter.org/

North American Association fro Environmental Education
http://eelink.net/pages/EE-Link+Introduction

SEEK
http://www.seek.state.mn.us/

Web of Creation
http://www.webofcreation.org/

Peace and Justice

Center for Children and Theology Nonviolence
https://cctheo.org/node/12

Sojourners: Christians for Justice and Peace
http://sojo.net/

Joint Religious Legislative Council
http://www.jrlc.org/

Christian Non-Violence Study Group
http://www.angelfire.com/mn2/peace/

United Nations Special Session on Children
http://www.unicef.org/specialsession/

UNICEF
http://www.unicef.org/

United Nations Children's News

http://www.irinnews.org/frontpage.aspx?SelectTheme=Children

Center for Research on Child Well Being
http://crcw.princeton.edu/

Future of Children
http://www.futureofchildren.org/

Spirituality

Association for Children's Spirituality
http://www.cwvp.com/

Media

Challenge of Media Culture
http://mhess/mrcsource.html

Film Study Sites
http://mhess/film.html

Mediawise
http://www.mediafamily.org

The Media Theory Site
http://www.theory.org.uk/

Internet Movie Database
http://www.imdb.com/

Movie Themes Index

http://www.textweek.com/movies/themeindex.htm

Movie Reviews
http://www.mrqe.com/lookup

Websites about films and faith
http://www.cmu.ca/library/faithfilm.html

Pop culture from a spiritual point of view
http://www.hollywoodjesus.com/

Christian Music Central
http://www.cmcentral.com/

Media Channel
http://www.mediachannel.org/

Media Literacy Websites
http://www.medialit.org/

Christian Software for children, youth and adults
http://www.sundaysoftware.com/

Leadership

Religion and Ethics News Weekly
http://www.pbs.org/wnet/religionandethics/

Resources for Christian Leaders
http://www.christianleaders.org/

Journal of Religious Leadership
http://www.christianleaders.org/JRL/index.htm

Pulpit and Pew Research on Pastoral Leadership
http://www.pulpitandpew.org/

Alban Institute
http://www.alban.org/

Lilly Endowment Religion page
http://www.lillyendowment.org/religion.html

Journal of Lutheran Ethics
http://www.elca.org/jle/

Resources for American Christianity
http://www.resourcingchristianity.org/

Mentoring Peer Resources
http://www.peer.ca/mentor.html

Mentoring
http://www.mentoring.org

Professional Religious Educational

Religious Education Association
http://www.religiouseducation.net/

Religious Studies Web Guide
http://www.acs.ucalgary.ca/~lipton/index.html

Hartford Institute for Religious Education
http://hirr.hartsem.edu/

Programs for the Theological Exploration of Vocation
http://www.ptev.org/

Wabash Center for Teaching and Learning in Theology and Religion
http://www.wabashcenter.wabash.edu/

Yale University Divinity School Library Research Guide for Christianity
http://web.library.yale.edu/

Reference Tools
http://guides.library.yale.edu/citationmanagement

Free Online Religion Resources
http://www.library.yale.edu/div/forfree.html

American Academy of Religion
https://www.aarweb.org/

Lutheran Association of Christian Educators
http://faithfulteaching.org/

Association of Presbyterian Church Educators
http://apcenet.org/

Resources and Publishers

Augsburg Fortress
http://www.augsburgfortress.org/

Group Publishing
http://www.group.com/

Hartcourt Religion Publishers: Whole Community Catechesis
http://www.harcourtreligion.com/wcc.asp

Cokesbury
http://www.ileadyouth.com/default.asp

Youthwork: resources for youth workers
http://www.youthwork.com/

Godly Play Resources
http://www.godlyplayresources.com/

Search Institute
http://www.search-institute.org/

Faith Inkubators
http://www.faithink.com/

Practicing Our Faith
http://www.practicingourfaith.org/

Youth and Family Institute
http://www.youthandfamilyinstitute.org

Christian Software for children, youth and adults
http://www.sundaysoftware.com/

Youth Leadership
www.youthleadership.org

Statistics About Children and Youth

AACAP developed Facts for Families to provide concise and up-to-date information on issues that affect children, teenagers, and their families
http://www.aacap.org/AACAP/AACAP/Families_and_Youth/Facts_for_Families/Home.aspx

Kids Count tracks the status of children in the country
http://www.aecf.org/MajorInitiatives/KIDSCOUNT.aspx

American Religion Data Archive-recent religious statistics are available
http://www.thearda.com/

Statistics about America's children
http://www.childstats.gov/americaschildren/index.asp

Child Trends Data Bank
http://www.childtrendsdatabank.org/

Bureau for Justice Statistics about juveniles
http://www.bjs.gov/index.cfm?ty=tp&tid=146

World Religions Statistic Geography Church Statistics
http://www.adherents.com/

The Health and Well-being of Children and Youth

Children's Defense Fund
http://www.childrensdefense.org/

The Future of Children provides resources and analysis to promote effective policies and programs for children from Princeton and Brookings Research
http://www.futureofchildren.org/

Viva Network: Better Care for Children
http://www.viva.org/?page_id=56
http://www.viva.org/?page_id=316

Annie E Casey Foundation to build better futures for vulnerable children and families
http://www.aecf.org

Children Now organization to ensure that children are at the top of public policy
http://www.childrennow.org/

Clearing House on Developments in Child, Youth and Family Policies
http://www.childpolicyintl.org/
http://www.childpolicy.org/

List of Crisis Hotlines from National Clearinghouse on
Families and Youth
http://www.ncfy.com/hotline.htm

Child and Family Web Guide for a multitude of issues for children
of all ages and families
http://www.cfw.tufts.edu/

American Academy of Child & Adolescent Psychiatry has resources
on many issues affecting children and youth
http://www.aacap.org/

List of websites for youth in crisis
http://www.cpyu.org/resources/

National PTA has good parent resources section
http://www.pta.org/

Children Youth and Family Consortium at U of M
http://www.cyfc.umn.edu/welcome.html

Frameworks Institute: Kids Count E-Zines articles about issues
involving children
http://www.frameworksinstitute.org/children.html

Childwatch CWI Research Resources: The network is a response of the research community to insure that the perspectives of children are heard.
http://www.crin.org/organisations/viewOrg.asp?ID=288

Children Youth and Families Education and Research Network
http://www.cyfernet.org/

Youthwork: resources for youth workers
http://www.youthwork.com/

Youth Today is an on-line newsletter about working with youth
http://www.youthtoday.org/

Become a Child Advocate
http://www.onlinepsychologydegree.net/2012/10/29/become-a-child-advocate/

Interfaith Websites

World Religions Index: a website to help Christians understand other world faiths
http://wri.leaderu.com/

Interfaith Network
http://www.nain.org/

Bibliography

Bancroft, Emery. *Christian Theology*. Grand Rapids: Zondervan, 1961.

Barna, George. *The Barna Report*. Glendale: Barna Research Group, Ltd., 1991.

_____. *The Future of the American Family*. Chicago: Moody Press, 1993.

_____. *The Invisible Generation: Baby Busters*. Glendale: Barna Research Group, Ltd., 1992.

_____. *The 1994 Churched Youth Survey*. Glendale: Barna Research Group, Ltd., 1994.

_____. *Today's Teens, A Generation in Transition*. Glendale: Barna Research Group, Ltd., 1991.

Bauer, Gary. *Our Journey Home*. Dallas: Word Publishing, 1992. Clark, Chad. *Next Time I Fall in Love*. Grand Rapids: Zondervan, 1993.

Courtney, Edward. *Family Awareness Program Manual.* Austin: Quest for Truth, 1993.

DePree, Max. *Leadership Jazz.* New York: Doubleday, 1992.

Engstrom, Ted W. *The Making of a Christian Leader.* Grand Rapids: Zondervan, 1976.

Fineman, Howard. "The Virtuecrats." *Newsweek,* 13 June 1994, 36.

Hendricks, Howard. *Teaching to Change Lives.* Portland: Multnomah Press, 1987.

_____. *The Seven Laws of Christian Leadership.* Philadelphia: Regal Books, 1991.

Hutchcraft, Ron. "Specific Challenges for Today's Youth." *Ministry Advantage 5* (July/August 1994): 12.

Johnson, Greg and Yorkey, Mike. *Faithful Parents, Faithful Kids.* Wheaton, 111.: Tyndale House, 1993.

Johnston, Ray. *Developing Spiritual Growth in Middle School Students.* El Cajon, Ca.: Youth Specialties, 1994.

Laurent, Robert. *Keeping Your Teen in Touch With God.* Elgin, 111.: David C. Cook, 1988.

Lenhart, Jennifer. "A Gun Is Power." *Houston Chronicle,* 14 August, 1994, Special Section, 12.

Liebrum, Jennifer. "Youth Will Be Tried as Adult in Bear Creek Death of Teen." *Houston Chronicle,* 14 August 1994, Special Section, 22.

Lloyd-Jones, D. Martyn. *Preaching and Preachers.* Grand Rapids: Zondervan, 1972.

Maxwell, John C. *Be A People Person.* Wheaton, IL: Victor Books, 1994.

McDowell, Josh and Hostetler, Bob. *Right From Wrong.* Dallas: Word Publishing, 1994.

McManus, Michael. 50 *Practical Ways to Take Our Youth Back from the World.* Wheaton, IL: Tyndale House, 1993.

Robbins, Duffy. *Going the Distance.* Grand Rapids: Zondervan, 1991.

Robinson, Haddon. *Biblical Preaching.* Grand Rapids: Baker Book House, 1980. Rowatt, G.

Wade, Jr. *How to Talk to Teenagers.* Nashville: Broadman Press, 1990. Smalley, Gary. *The Key to Your Child's Heart.* Dallas: Word Publishing, 1992.

Spader, Dann and Mayes, Gary. *Growing a Healthy Church.* Chicago: Moody Press, 1991.

Stanley, Charles. *How to Keep Your Youth On Your Team.* Nashville: Thomas Nelson, 1986.

Tolson, Mike. "Seeds of Trouble." *Houston Chronicle,* 14 August 1994, Special Section, 2.

Endnotes

Introduction

[1] George Barna, *The Future of the American Family* (Chicago: Moody Press, 1993), 98-99.

[2] Ron Hutchcraft, "Specific Challenges for Today's Youth," *Ministry Advantage* 5 (July/Aug 1994): 12.

Chapter 1

[1] Jennifer Liebrum, "Youth Will be Tried as Adult in Bear Creek Death of Teen," *Houston Chronicle,* 14 April 1994, Special Section, p. 22.

[2] Mike Tolson, "Seeds of Trouble," *Houston Chronicle,* 14 August 1994, Special Section, p. 2.

Chapter 2

[1] George Barna, *The 1994 Churched Youth Survey* (Glendale: Barna Research Group Ltd., 1994), pp. 10-11.

[2] Ibid., 12.

[3] Ibid., 12-13.

[4] Ibid., 14.

[5] Ibid., 15.

[6] Ibid, 16-18.

[7] Ibid, 18-19.

[8] Ibid., 19.

[9] Ibid., 19-20.

[10] Ibid., 21.

[11] Ibid., 21-22.

[12] Ibid., 22-23.

[13] Ibid., 23-24.

[14] George Barna, *Today's Teens: A Generation in Transition* (Glendale: Barna Research Group Ltg., 1991), 3-4.

[15] Ibid., 6-7.

[16] Ibid, 11.

[17] Ibid.

[18] Howard Fineman, "The Virtuecrats," *Newsweek,* 13 June 1994, 36.

[19] Ibid.

[20] Mike Tolson, "Seeds of Trouble," *Houston Chronicle,* 14 August 1994, Special Section, p. 14.

Chapter 3

[1] Jennifer Lenhart, "A Gun is Power," *Houston Chronicle,* 14 August 1994, Special Section, p. 12.

[2] Ibid.

Chapter 4

[1] Edward Courtney, *Family Awareness Program Manual* (Austin: Quest for Truth, 1993), 38.

[2] Haddon W. Robinson, *Biblical Preaching* (Grand Rapids: Baker Book House Co., 1980), 193.

[3] G. Wade Rowatt Jr., *How to Talk to Teenagers* (Nashville: Broadman Press, 1990), 39-58.

[4] Ibid., 45.

[5] Howard G. Hendricks, *Teaching to Change Lives* (Portland: Multnomah, 1987), 100.

[6] Ibid., 101-102.

Chapter 5

[1] Cited by Ray Johnston, *Developing Spiritual Growth in Middle School Students* (El Cajon, Ca.: Youth Specialties, 1994), 18.

[2] Edward Courtney, *Family Awareness Program Manual* (Austin: Quest for Truth, 1993), 13.

[3] Ibid., 19.

[4] Greg Johnson and Mike Yorkey, *Faithful Parents, Faithful Kids* (Wheaton: Tyndale House Publishing, 1993), 111.

[5] Courtney, 49.

[6] http://compassinterventions.com/alcohol-drug-statistics.html

[7] Ibid., 12.

[8] Ibid., 44.

[9] Ibid., 44-45.

Chapter 6

[1] John C. Maxwell, *Be A People Person* (Wheaton: Victor Books, 1994), 132.

[2] Howard G. Hendricks, *Teaching to Change Lives* (Portland: Multnomah Press, 1987), 63-66.

[3] Michael J. McManus, *50 Practical Ways to Take Our Youth Back From the World* (Wheaton: Tyndale House Publishers, 1993), 48.

[4] Ibid., 48-49.

[5] Gary Smalley, *The Key to Your Child's Heart* (Dallas: Word Publishing, 1992), 49-50.

[6] Ibid, 50-52.

[7] Ibid, 54.

[8] Ibid.

[9] Hendricks, *Teaching,* 51.

Chapter 7

[1] Ray Johnston, *Developing Spiritual Growth in Middle School Students* (El Cajon, CA: Youth Specialties, 1994), 105.

Chapter 8

[1] Cited by Robert Laurent, *Keeping Your Teen In Touch With God* (Elgin, III: David C Cook Publishing Co., 1988), 58.

[2] Gary Smalley, *The Key to Your Child's Heart* (Dallas: Word Publishing, 1992), 39-44.

[3] George Barna, *The Future of the American Family* (Chicago: Moody Press, 1993), 205.

⁴ Greg Johnson and Mike Yorkey, *Faithful Parents, Faithful Kids* (Wheaton: Tyndale House Publishing, 1993), 111.

⁵ Ibid., 113.

⁶ Ibid., 114-115.

⁷ Ibid, 116.

⁸ Ibid, 118.

⁹ Edward Courtney, *Family Awareness Program Manual* (Austin: Quest for Truth, 1993), 7-8.

¹⁰ Johnson and Yorkey, 119.

¹¹ Ibid., 120.

¹² Ibid, 121.

¹³ Ibid., 122.

¹⁴ Ibid., 123.

¹⁵ Barna, *Future,* 171-172.

¹⁶ *USA Today, June 19, 2009*

¹⁷ *Future*, 205.

Chapter 9

¹ George Barna, *The Future of the American Family* (Chicago: Moody Press, 1993), 208-209.

Chapter 10

¹ Gary Bauer, *Our Journey Home* (Dallas: Word Publishing, 1992), 190-192.

² Ibid., 47-48.

Chapter 11

[1] Gary Bauer, *Our Journey Home* (Dallas: Word Publishing, 1992), 43-44.

[2] Cited by Edward Courtney, *Family Awareness Program Manual* (Austin: Quest for Truth, 1993), p. 85.

[3] Ibid

[4] Ibid., pp. 86-87.

[5] Ibid., 88-89.

[6] Ibid, 89-90.

Chapter 12

[1] McDowell and Bob Hosteller, *Right From Wrong* (Dallas: Word Publishing, 1994), 11.

[2] Ibid., 74-76.

[3] Ibid., 80-84 [paraphrase].

[4] Ibid, 105-106.

[5] Ibid, 106-107.

[6] Ibid., 113.

Conclusion

[1] George Barna, *The 1994 Churched Youth Survey* (Glendale: Barna Research Group Ltd., 1994), p. 22.

[2] George Barna, *Today's Teens: A Generation in Transition* (Glendale: Barna Research Group Ltd., 1991), p. 6.

[3] Barna, *Survey,* 68.

[4] Ibid., 72.

Appendix A

[1] McDowell and Bob Hostetler, *Right From Wrong* (Dallas: Word Publishing, 1994), 8-17.

About the Author

John A. Gross is Pastor Emeritus of North Park Baptist Church in Houston, Texas, and past President of Singing Hills Youth Camp of Albuquerque, New Mexico.

North Park Baptist Church has been a leader on the North side of Houston, where Pastor Gross has been leader for the past thirty-eight years The church has recently gone through several a major building programs, moving almost ten miles to a beautiful, thirty-acre parcel of land North of downtown Houston. The property is covered with the beautiful native trees of South Texas. Huge oak trees and sprawling pecan trees cover the skyline. The church site is a picturesque scene with the old colonial church sitting back behind the large shade trees. Its 120-foot steeple, large white columns, and circle drive make it one of the most beautiful settings in South Texas. North Park has one of the most promising futures of any church in the south. Surrounded by thousands of lost and needy people, the church has dedicated itself with a mission's statement that it is our desire to "reach out to as many people as possible, lead them to Jesus Christ as personal Savior, help them determine the will of God for their life, and help them fulfill the will of God for their life." North Park is a progressive, evangelistic church reaching out to the whole world through its worldwide missionary effort.

Dr. John Gross was President of one of the most successful youth camps in all the nation. For several years he was director and overseer of the operation of the facility with programs that have reached literally thousands of young people. Young people have attended Singing Hills from all over the United States. Thousands have made decisions, accepting Christ as Savior. Many, many have made commitments of service throughout the years. Youth work has been a love of John, Susan his wife and their family through the years, and the Lord has truly blessed their efforts.

John is married to Susan and states in this project that she is his "best friend." The Grosses have two children—a son, John Thomas "Tommy" and a daughter, Debbie Lynne. Tommy's wife is Lynette and they have two children, Parker and Casie. Debbie and her husband Bill have two girls, Tiffany and Heather.

Pastor Gross attended Frank Phillips Junior College in Borger, Texas, and later transferred to Baptist Bible College in Springfield, Missouri, where he received a Th.G. in Theology, and then received a Bachelor of Theology Degree from Louisiana Baptist Seminary in Shreveport, Louisiana. He has taken courses from the University of Texas and completed his Doctor of Ministry at Bakke Graduate University in Seattle, Washington.

CPSIA information can be obtained
at www.ICGtesting.com
Printed in the USA
LVOW01s0418090216
474270LV00010B/126/P